"You can see it from the beginning when Rensberger first lays down his talent: the sharp eye, the life's dedication not to looking but to seeing, really seeing. It is here where a field in his daily walk is a "green wing of the hill" and "broken rooms [are] stacked with moonlight and shadow." It is here in the night where the young "fall on one another / in a tangle of cries of discovery" and "birds in black coats / minister to the newly dead." So when he says, "there is no barrier between my sleep and yours," who's to say he's not seeing in his mind's eye for me? Or for you?"

-Alice Friman, author of *The Overnight Train: New & Selected Poems*

"There is no / horizon, only leakage towards heaven," Eric Rensberger tells us in his astonishing *Notes to Self: Selected Poems*—a leak toward heaven Rensberger engages in a volume that captures his decades of poetic excavations. He digs deep into the soil of his everyday Indiana roots, where he grew up and has lived most of his life, giving us a body of work that breathes into the earth and through it with the wise eyes of someone who "knows" yet presents himself as just another "learner." He tells us, self-depracatingly, "Five buzzards on the lawn, all related to me"; yet we know his heart, one that embraces the missteps of our lives as a gift: "the mistakes in music / are not shameful / they are another music coming in." Some mistakes enter through trusting language: "it was strange but / I was stranger / I meant to say strong but strange will do." With such generative slippages, Rensberger displays a kinship with poets who embrace the world's fluidity as a form of redemption. His brand of "regionalism" is never narrow but springs from the particular, moving beyond mere geography into insights that are wide-ranging. What he discovers is a selfless self that seeks understanding through a practice of deep attentiveness to the world— and how the outer world connects to the inner. As he tells us in "Summit": after i cut / the apple / i had to / treat both / halves fairly." Rensberger's poems "cut" into his own heart and into the heart of the world simultaneously, seeking balance. It is a cutting that is always preparing itself to heal. In "Poem of Water," his goals are clear, tender, and beautiful: "I want to be a different kind of water / in a bed of horizons with other waters." Here is a poet who speaks to and from our most secret selves. *Notes to Self* is a remarkable achievement, a book I will return to again and again—a book we all need, whether or not we know it!"

-George Kalamaras, former Poet Laureate of Indiana

NOTES TO SELF:
SELECTED POEMS

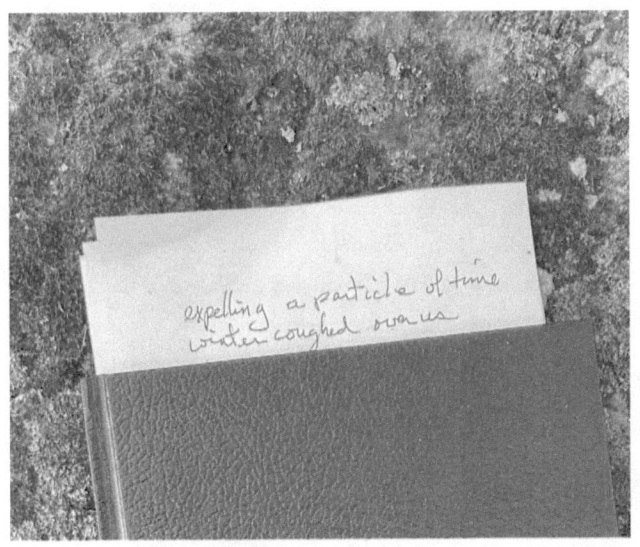

Eric Rensberger

Luchador Press
Big Tuna, Texas

Copyright © Eric Rensberger, 2025
First Edition: 1 3 5 7 9 10 8 6 4 2
ISBN: 978-1-958182-98-7
LCCN: 2025937981

Cover image: Eric Rensberger
Author photo: Rich Remsberg

Acknowledgments

The idea for this collection has been on my mind for several years, but it would not have come into existence without the help and encouragement of Tony Brewer. I also want to express my gratitude for the supportive environment and feedback provided by the members of the Writers Guild at Bloomington. I am sure that it has made my writing stronger to be part of a community of other writers. In this regard I should also mention the collection of poets who constituted the Bloomington Poetry Workshop in the 1980s. Finally, for his attentive reading and useful comments over many years, I want to warmly thank Elijah Pritchett, my most constant audience.

Table of Contents:

From LETTERS (1981)

From STANDING WHERE SOMETHING DID (1984)

From JOURNALISM (1984)

From BLANK OF BLANKS

ACCOUNT OF MY DAYS From AMD #1

From AMD #2

From AMD #3

From AMD #4

From AMD #5

From AMD #6

From AMD #7

From AMD #8

From AMD #9

From AMD#10

From AMD #11

From AMD#12

From AMD#13

From AMD #14

From AMD #15

From AMD #16

From AMD #17

From AMD#18

From AMD#19

From AMD#20

From AMD#21

From AMD #22

From AMD#23

From AMD#24

From AMD#25

From AMD#26

INTRODUCTION

Some of these poems were written in haste. That means some were not. Take everything I say with a twist.

The bulk of this book is selected from *Account of My Days*, an ongoing chronological collection. By "ongoing" I mean I keep writing them, or I have kept writing them, having no idea when I will stop. By "chronological" I mean placed in the order they began, even if the beginning is two words sitting together in an otherwise blank space.

I hate the idea that they could be taken as some kind of diary, as though you reading them could believe that I writing them believed in being able to keep an accurate and truthful record. Long ago, I noticed that my local library uses the common system of keeping poetry in the Nonfiction section. Being in nonfiction does not mean, "Everything in here is true." Just take a look at the history books.

I begin this collection with selections from chapbooks I published in the 1980s. The first poems in *Account of My Days* were written in 1985, in the midst of or off to one side of the chapbook production. My website, ericrensbergerpoetry.net, is the whole from which these parts are taken. In the introduction to the website, I have written "I am a local poet. I write Local Poetry. Much of it is about the weather. Like the weather, you may enjoy some, none, or all of it."

This now strikes me as a vain and evasive description. But I do write Local Poetry. Everyone does.

George Oppen says in one of his poems something along the lines of "my apprenticeship in that it was long was honorable." I have always understood this as a hint that you should never assume that your apprenticeship is over. I have gained much from encounters with other writers who have generously offered critiques, shown me their works, or said something in casual conversation that I took to use in a poem. Maybe I stole a line from somebody here and there, too.

If you are reading this, I have the firm belief you will have the patience to at least flip through a few pages to look at the poems. I welcome you and I sincerely hope to please. You are the one I have been writing for all along. I don't know you, but I have been writing for you all along.

for my parents

*The mind is the cause of our distresses
but of it we can build anew.*

-William Carlos Williams

LETTERS (1981)

Dear Eric,

The world could fall to pieces with no notice.
Imagine the nations sizzling under bombs big as
buildings, or submission and blood become the
whole of politics. Picture some bastard microbe
creeping amongst the billions dispelling ease.

Personal life, too, can come apart in disaster. Awful
car wrecks and stupid accidents will happen no
matter what. You might be the one to mishandle a
chainsaw or powerline. A hellbent vengeful hoodlum
in some cheap and raucous bar might knife you by
mistake.

Our advice is limited but wholesome. Don't go
anywhere in your car. Keep low when you walk and
stay close to cellars and holes. Sterilize your food.
Better yet, pack your car with gauze, climb in, have
it lowered to the bottom of a hole. Wait there till
you hear from us.

-The Wise

Dear Eric,

A chicken is a touchy creature. They scatter with dust and feathers and squawking at almost any noise. High-strung, dumb, stinking of ammonia, they peck at their cage corners with nervous pride.

Also, they die a lot. When I was drinking heavy and raising chickens, I found the daily burden of dead birds a hindrance to my thirst. I stopped digging single graves and began tossing fowl bodies into my empty silo. Mass burial. Once a week (Sundays) I'd get drunk and stick my head in, mingling words of hope and comfort with mournful bird-like chirps.

Well, anyway, you know how sick I got after I sold the farm. Swollen and weak, I finally had to give up even my beer. And, of course, your Dad would have called you by now to let you know I'm dead. I just thought I'd write to tell you that I got to heaven after all and it's not such a bad place. The walls and streets are lined with golden bottles of Miller's, and the angels come flying by with silver trays of whiskey, singing hosannas. Best of all, there's not a damn chicken anywhere.

-Uncle Al

from STANDING WHERE
SOMETHING DID (1984)

Busride

We are rolling. Snow and stubble
fields all around, vision bleaker
than I can tell. There is no
horizon, only leakage towards heaven
of vapors the earth becomes.
I haven't traveled this way
in years, not since I was broke
and twenty, but this kind of riding
stays the same and I can feel myself slipping
towards fourteen years ago
each time the blackbirds
step up from corn rows
into air. Pinions clatter, cold
pinches skin delicate as grass. They carry
their hunger with them in flight . . .
Your face had the same oval
my lips make closing towards a vowel.
Its shape goes everywhere with me
thin as paper.

You Know

You know who
was here. Wanted
the same old things.
I did what
you might expect,
considering. You can probably guess
what happened next.

R.T.

went out of
his mind
and saw his face
on every body

couldn't leave the street
(so taken
with the crowd).

HERBAL

Call it Cleavers, Jupiter's Nut,
Old Maid's Nightcap, Weazel Snout,
Key of Heaven, Adonis, Bugbane, or
Upright Virgin's Bower. Say that it's
striated, herbaceous, pyramidal,
has pendulous panicles. Use an
extract, infusion, poultice,
decoction, mouthwash, or gargle for
obstinate skin eruptions,
gout,
earache, nausea, ringworm,
languid indigestion
and flatulence.
A caution: though it is a
fine, cleansing, jovial plant,
very fragrant when bruised,
it converts the Rhenish wine to
insanely exhilarating Muscatel,
stupefies fish, and if eaten by birds
will tinge their bones red.

MY ANCESTORS

My ancestors abound within me:
one of them was stupid.
Fields pressed down with a mat of grasses,
houses squatting to spread lawns,
bright clover right up to the fence,
made him think he knew where his place was
like a beast coming up to its stall
satisfied. He had warm sides, an open mouth,
and a hollow place in the head
he filled up with devotion and trust,
simple trust, a trust so stupid
he thought the world
was always and everywhere a blessing.

THE TEMPTATION

The tree was hollow and I
stepped inside. The good round enclosing
shut me in. I heard what
an oak hears in the damp halfdark I chose.

Skin grows in rings, eyes
bark over, voice becomes a windy
mutter. Sap like slow
dynamite finds the secret brain.

Lay at my feet the food or
ornament you think will call
me out. My joints are knobs
of years and will not move.

from JOURNALISM (1984)

EYEBROWS

you can see your mustache,
the end of your nose, never me

face always the same
way

you think i am sensitive

two cats head to head
also like
stroking along the grain

IMPOSSIBLE

"the politician must have a
clear mental grasp of his constituency"

must please his lieutenants
with gifts of oranges, cashmere,
impossible jokes
his house
must have plenty of crawl space

SUMMIT

after i cut
the apple
i had to
treat both
halves fairly

from BLANK OF BLANKS (1988)

(AGAINST SILENCE)

In every direction
out of yourself
the page is scrambled.
While you work
blue shadows trace
across the pasture
huge outlines of trees.
Your arm is weakened by labor
your fingers darken
giving everything.

And it is necessary
when words fail
and syllables buzz
around your brain
with the arrogant
persistence of flies
to be swift and savage
catching them.

LIFE

no one survives it

MYSTERY

I found the murdered man's _____ in my hand
I left town
I went very fast
I was not tired from my effort
I became remarkable
I was pictured moving with a weather front
I stormed out of myself
I spoke, and my words were hail
I slowed down over the ocean
I sank
I could still run, but more heavily
I found the bottom
I buried my hand
the fish had eyes like search lights

ACCOUNT OF MY DAYS
from AMD#1

BLUE TWEED WITH FLECKS

for J.D.

Help in unlikely places
after the dirty pavement, the long drive,
artists bruising themselves with pink and acid green,
swimming pool of dark fins and bleeding lights,
doctors with paper hands, the intuitional labor,

a languorous thumping through the walls
(the old couple at it again
but blaming the noise on you),
help

from sitting still,
relief with your glass of wine
and my voice telling you
whatever comes next
your jacket with its flecks of color
is perfect.

TWELVE USES OF AN ABANDONED SPIDERWEB

it can be removed with a gesture
it does not threaten me with spiders
it gathers dust I can't be bothered with
it reveals by its subtle movements
it does what it has done
it is slight and receptive
it catches flies

(since the spider is gone the flies can escape
    if they struggle hard and their entrapment
    is not their own)

it has no insistent line
it is veins for a body of air
it becomes its shadows
it persists

MEN

The sale barn: sweat, cigars,
sawdust, four or five kinds
of manure. In the tight amphitheater
of rising benches, I stand next to my father,
not knowing any other place to be
and not wanting to be young enough
to be seen holding his hand.
This is where the men are,
with the animals. They march them
through the ring — sheep, pigs, cows —
and the auctioneer's "down biddadown"
sings dispassionately from behind a counter
set high so he can see everything.
His microphone is condensed
lightning, his messengers and bid-takers
run about the room, and at his right hand
sits a man with glasses, keeping accounts.
Above, the big blades of the ceiling fan
split the air into four parts. There are men
with long beards, men with smoking mouths,
men with wrists thick as my leg. I take
it all in, through my eyes, my nose,
I think I even take it in through my skin.

IMPERFECT POEM

I have nothing to say to you now
and nowhere to go to say it
I say nothing to you in my living room
and it's not right so I stand on the porch
and say nothing but the cows are there
listening so it doesn't seem like nothing
so I drive to town and walk down Kirkwood
saying nothing and it all feels wrong and
I'm out of place out of any place to walk
or stand or sit or lie down in peace
and it's like a death or the loss
of some essential organ without which
I don't see or hear and I can't feel my legs
and therefore I don't believe in the ground
which leaves me floating legless headless
bodiless anywhere everywhere this
must be what it's like to exist
in a world of no objects only ideas
that cannot be altered
the Platonic Heaven
goddamn you Plato you know
nothing about what it takes to be
in my life and be happy it takes
real flawed objects and people who can
be taken to represent nothing higher
or better or more perfect than themselves

SIDE WALK

Between the streetlamps there are regions of dark. You can't see anything, your vision melts away to nothing. I want to help — I always want to help — and in the murk I get to be cautious. Caution is one of my strongest traits, I'm very good at it, and here it is helpful. "Curb coming," I say, or "step up," or "the sidewalk is a little rough here." I take your elbow, I walk so close to you that our thighs brush and we have to establish a mutual rhythm. My caution now spreads out like the light from the streetlamps, and I worry what we look like. I am in a car on the street and I see two men walking in an embrace. Do I turn my head not to see, do I point the car at them, do I become excited? I am almost entirely caution now, and I have spread myself up and down the street. I am in all the houses, peeking out the windows scandalized in each of my secretive living rooms. I hold my breath, dangerous to myself. I want to help. I want to help.

LANDSCAPE: WEATHER BECOMING DOLPHY

evidence of high wind
everything that gets so far off the earth
is returned to it thrown down
new growth starts up
the bones of what did tower

/and the animals get their backs and rumps roughed up
    from bowing backward to the gale
/and the birds are made to skim an arm's length ahead
    of the storm
/and the people are built with extra bracing, like houses
    that expect the worst

and what's out there
the weather
is the same as what's
in every human heart
bad trouble and energy
enough to make it real

/but over there on the edge of the earth is a black wood
    with extra-human sounds in it
/and if the animals and the bent trees keep pointing in
    the right direction
/and if only the wind can reach that far and then blow
    through it and if

the right fingers appear
with their silver keys
unlocking faster and wider
than the wind can
slam shut the doors of
the wood, we'll finally hear

Dolphy before his head burst
playing how to live
between out and inward weather
and what's so beautiful about it
after all, what's so
important about someone
pulling melody after melody
out of his bountiful mouth

THE STRANGER

Him, the stranger walking toward you, he's the one you take into your heart. The rhythm of his stride becomes your pulse, you can feel it pumping through your shoulders, your neck, your eyes. Coming closer, you observe his waist and the shape of his hands. His face you've already memorized. You examine the surges of feeling within you and notice, surprised, that desire and courage are rooted to the same place. As he passes, you wonder if he realizes how much a part of you he is, you wonder if he has seen you, and decide that now (yes!) is the time to speak.

SHOPPING

It is important to tie your shoelaces — both shoelaces — before going into the pawn shop. And to carry only old bills, used till they have a softness like cloth. Take a friend. Just inside the door there are micrometers for measuring what you find. In a corner, there is talk cool as a silver flute to be had for next to nothing. Over there, a set of memories of red hair, slightly out of chronological order. A shelf containing the possibilities of loss: numbness, sorrow, fury, relief. Behind the counter, more talk — is flight too late, does the future have more pasts than the past has futures? A box with a broken latch is filled with a jumble of pages torn from calendars, each with at least one name, some with an X drawn through the date. As you leave, untie your shoelaces, check your pockets to make sure you are taking nothing home that is not yours.

NAKED AGAIN

It's night and I'm naked again
so there is no barrier between my sleep and yours,
I come to you nakedly to tell you
your dreams are real,

you do have to wash away the green clay of our making
outdoors, before thousands,
you do have to tell your father it makes no difference
that he sleeps with a woman younger than you,
though it does — and when you tell yourself
they can do as they please, you'll just watch TV,
you must realize the TV is in the bedroom with them,

and when you say never mind I'll smoke some pot,
you must remember they have the pot, too,
and when you rise, you will see
a man with a shaven head wearing a black skirt,
he is dancing on one foot but he does not spill his coffee,
he is singing his dream, which is of being told
to accept the manifold true ways of the Buddha,
he is joyous that he has awakened and does not
have to accept this or any other dream as true, he begs
to remind you, though, that the decision is ours,

to accept or not to accept, and it is made nakedly,
standing on the green clay, there will be footprints,
they will harden in the sun and hold forever the pattern,
the point of balance can be seen and the joint that carries
the heaviest weight, the callouses are outlined clearly,
but who will be there to read them?

POEM OF WATER

I want to be a different kind of water
in a bed of horizons with other waters

taste of salt taste of light

waves drown themselves
back to life

I am combing my hair and it shines
around my ears
my legs dissolve me forward

pouring over you I seek your
everywhere and I take away
saying nothing nothing

once in a rage I quit myself

if I fall on you without warning
close your eyes
they're beautiful

from AMD #2

NIGHT CREATURES

under the devious arch of the night
the MBA students are walking at the marshy edges of
    the lake with books in their hands
fat books books of promise and regret
long listings of fevers found money bruises good tests
    evil tests insults complaints answered money with
    no work hair growing where you don't want it
the students are weary of their studies
they look out over the dark mirror of the lake
and long for some reflection of their lives and labor
they listen to the little frogs crying for love
they stand in the mud of the shore and think of the
    earth extending herself
under the lake bearing the heavy burden of water
    without difficulty
wearing the lake like a hat
they adjust their ties and try to think the thoughts the
    earth would have under her hat of water

they no longer burn with wanting and planning and waiting
they are not blown here and there by the greater power of
    older men
the books fall from their hands and they feel this is it
the moment has come to abandon their fixed desires
to desire everything all at once
their haunches grow heavy they squat in the mud
this is the night of their true getting and spending
and the arch of the night no longer seems devious
it is an invitation to love and they fall on one another
in a tangle of cries of discovery

AUTOBIOGRAPHY

first I died
then I made a breakfast
of oranges and the joints of lambs

I stepped out into my new world
it was the old world too

the capital city of sorrow
where people lie
to each other every day
and the stones of the houses
crumble to dust at night

their river cuts through
from past to more distant past
it is a street
they ride sadly
without oars or an idea of oars

I reached childhood
I was alone
I decided not to cry
I had no mouth
and my feet always stumbled

I TRY BUT

you won't leave me alone
your name is on everyone's lips
the letter I sent out
comes back a judge invites me
to consider again the basic fact

you are written in my palm
I stick it in my pocket and
the keys jump I wash it
the water stays in the sink

if I went out driving
I would always be between
the road ahead the road behind
if I came back
I would not ask the reason

LAMENT

Is now the time to praise
things that need praising,
or to put right what has been
misused? The reign might
be long but it exhausts itself.
The people of one land seek another.
What strong hands put up
an evil wind wrecks easily,
within an hour the well-founded house
falls. Emptiness swallows
the beautiful faces, rings drop
from shrunken joints,
the bronze bells no longer sound,
and we are left to praise
things that need praising.

I COULD FALL OVER

Always losing patience with
myself I cross out and start over.
Always picking a dry rock
I follow the river foothold
by foothold. Always dipping
my hands into the cold
rush of water I bless away
my sadness and make light
gestures of lost handshakes.

Any way I lean I could
fall over. Emptiness paid
his call and left with you.
He represents a future
that eats itself. Always
looking for what I have left
in the cracks between stones,
the fall of fast water,
the separate noises of birds.

POEM ENDING WITH MY NAME

I watch TV.
It doesn't happen.

I make dinner.
It doesn't happen.

I answer the phone,
I change my clothes,
I smoke my pipe,
I sit on the couch.

It doesn't happen.

I get sleepy.
There is a knock at the door.

Someone says Eric.

BELIEVING IN A HIDDEN ENEMY

I went up the stairs in the dark.
I was trying for the one door
that opens outward.
That sharp noise outside —
it could be anything
I am ashamed of.

The world has become
a closed circle I can set
on my finger, and when I scratch
its ridges a voice springs out
of the quiet with names
and praise and condemnation.

It is a dark place I live in
and I like it. Who would
you be, downstairs in
my living room, and why
do you not stumble? It is
a dark place, and you don't stumble.

untitled

I will marry my blear eye to a blind eye
standing with the reverends of the dark
and hooting with them in the canopy of trees
lit by the electricity of my nerves the black shadows
of all my thoughts carried to their extreme conclusions

I will send my eyes off on a journey with farewells
unceasing and fading waves of the hand
they will see and they will not see what I tell them
and cover their shame with lace and bathe
in goldenseal and eyebright bayberry bark and raspberry

and in the hotel of my skull occupy the finest floor
the waiters will run to them with outstretched hands
to give and receive and press against muscles
of a back tired of loving tired of play
tired of the upright posture of the merely sighted

SUGGESTION

Let the poets die
spiraling in their heavy overcoats
down from some built miracle
above the heads of men

or in their beds
blanketed with age
and infirm but
sending their living part
upward passing
but never intercepting
the poets' bodies falling

Let them select death
as a stanza to be filled
with muttering
which is almost words
or once was words

Let them look up
or down once twice
the look that precedes us
everywhere we go

search of landscapes
for old gods plea
for money arrow
of desire

Let them feel the dry itch
in the throat fame waters
but never satisfies
like death the
distinguished thing
the last word
closing the door
on fingers that held the pen
and steadied the paper

FIVE SEASONS

King Curtis blows his
Soul Serenade. Summer daisies
and junebugs in — second night
of heat. Crickets and whippoorwill
calling, stars steady, high.
Below, fireflies dance
the treetops, then take
the trunks down, spread out
through the pasture.
Love blinks as if random, as if
everywhere. The sax blows
and trills and blows.
There is a dark no one sees
but you. Eyes open, eyes closed.
Five seasons, and then you go.

SKETCH

In the dark the boy
lies on his sheets light
as windrows of hay
on stubble. The smell
of cut hay comes through
one window and goes out
the other. The President
of Icebergs has sent us
a small cool breeze,
the one he could spare.
The boy's damp skin,
his wakefulness,
his unimaginable
years to come.

SENTENCE

A restaurant where you are left alone
with your hunger, where the chef
has cut off his hands and served them
to a dog with no teeth, where the waiter
avoids your eyes because of the suffering
in them (he can stand suffering no more),
where everyone looks beautiful but you
so instead of a tip you leave your eyes,
where they do not take reservations, in fact
they pretend they are never open,
and the street is closed for repairs, for
repairs repented, broken, and done again.

HE SAID

everything mastered him
each step felt

like helpless
falling

what he did
for love

with no one
looking

but me
the time he

always lost
waiting

his turn
to be first

the way the world
filled up

after him
like a wound

healing
from inside

THE UNLOVED BELOVED

"The Unloved Beloved" is written by the crazy son of the man who teaches the masculine arts in the back of his hardware store. Everybody takes his classes, for he never shames his students for their difficulties. He even forgives the one who stole a Winchester propped against a wall in the rain with a "please don't steal me" sign on it. He needs help. His fishing lines are tangled, and he wants reassurance about his son, who is supposed to be good at what he does, though his father does not understand. What the man seeks from the thief is confirmation that his son does well, that he is famous, which is the kind of information only a thief would have. The man and the thief walk downstairs together, not where the police can see them but behind all the activity in the store and mercifully far away from the other students. "He takes up a lot of space," the thief says. "I mean, more than just his own." He wants the man to be pleased, but he has never understood such men, and he fears his comment will be taken poorly, so the thief turns to the man and smiles and tries to make a joke of it. He must not piss off the one man who could explain him to himself in such a way that he could see he is not a thief, that what he's done is entirely acceptable to the teacher of masculine arts.

from AMD #3

NO MISTAKES

understand me: I am the musician
who has come to blows
with music   heading into
a mirror I adjust the darkness
before my eyes and believe
that with the god in me
no mistakes will be made

over and above the drums
I lay the experience of my mouth
wetness and tension
and out of the gravity
I carry always comes the weight
that makes me fall swiftly
into myself finding

the drop that takes me
to mean more than I
ever am   believe me
I'm back in a corner I don't know
I made and it's good to learn
what no one teaches that you can
give up as a way of getting out

FINDING

my eyes if I should lose them
would find this paper
and look for your name

its shape unlike its sound

written in black on which eyes
can rest forever because their centers
are perfect blackness silent robust

your name if I should lose it
would be everyone's name
and I would recognize you
without eyes

AGAINST IMMORTALITY

I don't want to live forever
I don't want to be taken out of my dying body
I don't want to be more enduring than the hills
their purple color flecked with orange
the black spot of buzzard hanging high above
seeing many hilltops at once
smelling all the threads of scent autumn sends up

the change of weather coming
across the horizon's expanding age
changes in the wind the moisture the order of stars
and change below smaller
sometimes furtive things slowing or stopping
flesh now unmoving slackening richly
giving off its scent of decay

like a beacon of light to the mind
of a buzzard a point around which
one can swirl on wide wings and feel
how the point can dim but while it still
lasts can be the center and inspiration
of a spiral closing in on itself
with the fullness of an apple holding her seeds

PROTESTANT MEMORY

to keep myself from crying
I recall my birth
in the old township

the fields were rich
grain had poured in to church
till the pews were buried

and the preacher sat on top
choking from the dust but still
leading the singing

his tenor so clear the air parted
and the dead walked through
the Egypt of their memory pursuing

we took them into our bellies
folded their voices between
the leaves of our new hymnals

sanctuary so welcome
they stayed after for the potluck
and the blessing of infants

RELIGIOUS SCENE

on the wall of the steakhouse
next to the taxi building
someone has painted Leonardo's
Last Supper in bright colors

Jesus and His disciples
are threatened by the creeper
growing heavily over the bricks
and now it's raining so

they are wet and the creeper
is coming and the cabdrivers
are irritable and half-crazy
and all the disciples are shocked

by what Jesus has just said
while the buses rolled past
the most innocent one thinks
the rumble made him misunderstand

he would do anything would
even give his soul to help
the Master have what He pleased
how could he do what is intended?

those less innocent are eager
to explain away the misunderstanding
Not on my life No I'd never
trying to convince each other you see

ON MY CARPET

he calls it his
fake leg
says you have to
get used to falling

but at least now
he can drive
a stick shift

a leaf came in
on his shoe
and stayed here
I like its color and
suggestion of weather

AS HE SHIFTS THEM

In the back pew of
The Unknowable Church of Christ
Jesus waits for the children's choir to sing
so He can pull the ivory cubes
from His pocket with their clicks
unheard

His lips are moving and you might think
He's singing along but really He's saying
should I play dice or shouldn't I
as He shifts them from one fist to the other

12/31/91

outside in
dark air
ghosts flirt
each other

the year that
came so grand
in is gone
I sit close

to the weak
lamp and read
my poems
outside one

ghost whispers
in another's ear
they belong
to themselves

only or
to themselves
and the gone
year the new

year passes
through their hearts
and they feel
nothing

ROCK PAINTING

the dance I did
out of time
quick as a flea

your minor key eyes
caught me
my ten fingers

pointed ten
different ways

NIGHTWORK

the secret government
of the United States
meeting in a doughnut shop
at 2:00 a.m. disguises

killers as countergirls and
busboys to guard
the door and see
that they are alone

which done they begin
singing and passing money
around the room
the more they sing

the faster the money
is handed around
the quicker the money goes
the louder the song

soon they are dancing
and flinging bundles
of bills at each other
the blinds are closed

they sweat their arms
ache their throats are
sore but the song
and dance go on

till just before the
first customers are
expected stopping
on their way to

their shitty early
morning jobs no one
could like or really
want to keep

the blinds open
dark figures shuffle away
the killers are replaced
by the real help

and one sleepy guy
coming in stumbles —
what luck! — on
a pile of money

ODE TO THE FRIENDS OF POETRY

the friends of poetry
are in trouble
they have not held their tongues
they lose their jobs
they are criticized for too much hair
or no hair
their parents despair
their friends lament

no one understands them
if they climb a ladder
someone says don't jump
if they go to the cellar
to check the furnace
someone says there is
a bomb being made down there

their friends tap their temples
their lovers sigh
there are police cruisers
out looking for the uncontrolled
the believers in vice and havoc
those who have been given clear choices
and reject what all others take

the poets themselves are out
looking for the friends of poetry
don't take it so much to heart
don't hurt yourself
look it's not worth it
keep your job keep your
mouth shut I have to
live with it so can you

but the friends of poetry
never listen to the poets
it's the poems they hear and obey
no matter how strange it makes them
how alone hunted afraid
else why
have listened in the first place

from AMD #4

ABOUT TO SIT DOWN

Stepping out the back door
and watching snow settle
bright gleaming on the woodpile,
the backwards and forwards
looking guy smells smoke,
and the color of the leaf-covered
ground comes up into his eyes.
Daylight is going to bed in
the dirt, and snowflakes follow it
as far down as they can. The backwards
and forwards looking guy
is about to sit down and remember
all the snows he can and imagine
the ones to come. He leans back
in the rocker and releases,
his weight impelling its own motion
the other way. If my youth
were a summer pasture I'd be in
a migration now toward
the lower slopes, just ahead of winter.
He sniffs his own smoke and
thinks I'm burning too
but slowly enough
to be good for me.

KISS HIS EAR

Brown corn bends as
gusts knock things around,
sky gets close enough
to share her rain
on the late-green hill pastures:

this misplaced spring storm
in the middle of winter, wind's
wiggle up the spine of the ridge
I ride on with Jeremiah Van Gogh,
who won't share his vision
unless you tell him he's crazy

and kiss his ear. Meanwhile
birds in black coats
minister to the newly dead
with beaks like scars and speak
a biography that sounds
like hunger.

FIELD GUIDE

indigo bunting no words
distinct enough for the blue
brilliance with touches of dark
(not black more like pieces
of shade stuck to face
wingtips tail as its flights
bounce through the borders of
the woods) nor for the character
expressed in its peck at the seed
spread on the common board
of the porch rail or its
other discreet choices of
association with the world
we have built is it vanity
and false sentiment that makes us
claim the completion of creation
is our noticing of it? while
the bunting simply needs seed
and there is nothing remarkable
enough for it to have learned
language only song

untitled

I knew
if I said to you
the words that burned me
you would swallow them
and they would be in you
a hunger so great
it would like love
make you want
to draw me into your mouth

I STAY UP LATE

studying to live
within the law also

practicing excuses
it is midnight

the page is dim it
might be a desert

no one has traveled
the words are spiders

who would follow
spiders no matter

how beautiful their
plan or how much

water they catch
from the air with it

and in a desert
there is no law

but necessity so
to whatever I yield

I am innocent

untitled

underground I'll turn to you
bones won't matter
only after I could act
did I understand them

here the evidence we've lied
is safe we can share it
without being taken away
(nothing will take us away)

if I pour you a drink
my hands will be dry
if we don't try to escape
we won't get lost

THEFT OF A LINE FROM TATE

I consider it a citizen's duty
I'm unfit for another awful
citizen's night of choking on my own throat
I want to avoid if the room doesn't
stink I want to know why
but maybe that's my mother talking
what I've been thinking is
what I've been up to is justified
by the bruises I've collected
and the animals I haven't even seen
much less sent off to the zoo

HOW I TRAPPED THE MURDERER

I left out the part
about Death, the finite details
that would have given me away.
I wept as though I were remorseful
and swung onto my back
the heavy bag someone had to carry.
I washed my hands till they bled.
The blue jays' song chiseled away
at my innocence, so I backed up
the others' alibis though no one
had heard of mine. If it was up
to anyone to confess then it was
time for everyone to surrender:
hands in the air, walking in a line —
it was like dancing, and I led.

PROVERB

he who sleeps a false sleep
is a storm locked in a house
drinks from a glass of obscurity

bored silent rejecting
this hour and the next
he hides what he has stolen

where it is sure to be found
his religion is to trust nothing
by prayer he means setting fires

I AM PART BUZZARD

my grandmother was a buzzard
she had two sisters
one was mad
one was smart
no one knew which
the short one
gave me a mandolin
or rather I took it
when she died

INTERRUPTION

not knowing what to say
my mind won't turn to it
I offer some elaborate compliment
instead of tears
I refuse to believe
in your going

these flowers for instance
I picked them from my garden
and from the wild edges
of the woods I live in
they open themselves to me
though I'm not a bee
or hummingbird

why would they
offer to me
color form and fragrance
why would I take them
if anything at all would interrupt
their beauty and my savoring

BLUE MILLION

in the house dark
with echoes a fire
starts up and the echoes

crowd around
circulating a joke
that sounds like footsteps

in the fluttering light
your face appears
reflecting something

that went through
the house a blue
million times

went through my house
so many echoes
the fire the dark

my unforgotten one
your effortless eyes
and so long shoes

AUTOBIOGRAPHY VOL. II

the day before my birth
I was in my house in the woods
everything was ready

I had my soul in my pocket
I stood before the mirror
in my white suit

am I awakened yet
doubting the hour of my liberation

mother's heart was thumping
marriage had been a mistake
the heat was terrible
would this birth be easier

I straightened myself
checked the time
reached in my pocket and found

a stone I had gathered
by the smoothing sea
its edges taken tide by tide

in my palm the spotted mass
flecks like black mirrors

I bent close
my face is in each speck
this must be the soul
I was looking for

from AMD #5

untitled

some words last longer
than dressed stone
you have these
all that's left
of me and my difference

and my other
difference and my —

I've wedged
what would fit here
lip of human wisdom's
deep well

where a frog sits boasting
to the black night
and bright stars

MEMORY

noon the infinite
noises of bugs
jug of cold water
we baled up
summer till
all the fields
were empty

TITLE NO TITLE

if your hand
carried me to your eyes
and your eyes carried
water to wash me

if your hand your eyes
were nothing new
and the kiss was old
and the tongue didn't

set off its dynamite
would the blood still
have what it needed
oxygen and divinity

NOTICING

how to be literal as a last gasp

how moonlight sticks in your hair

how fingers melt into the things they pry open

how to get into your clothes without dropping your
    nakedness

how the hills fill up with water till the trees drown and
    small farms and graves sink to the bottom

how objects stay close to their shadows for fear of being
    parted forever

how this fear is like a lake that fills up the hills and we
    could drown in it

except that our voices keep calling out the strokes that keep
    us afloat and listening to each other we know

how to strike out for shore and leave the raft to its other
    extreme

LOOKOUT

looking out from a window in the treetops
where just this morning a host of blackbirds
came through moving from branch to branch
never stopping only resting a minute then
flying off through the fog over our ripple in the hills

their calls to each other were unceasing they held
the flock together and not one stayed behind
a few minutes and they were gone but left
some shit a few unnecessary feathers and a chill
in the heart since their passing seemed a warning

MONEY WORRIES

dreaming of an owl
hooting in my face
waking late to a low sky
gray withholding light
fire to build Sunday morning
network news shows with
politics and personal vignettes
of the ordinary middle hearted
starvation we can plan for

the road is gray as the sky
it only pretends to go
where I'm going I only
go there to get money
the violence of the storm
descends till it reaches earth
which it cannot toss about
your troubles your troubles
my troubles the wind's

power is in its voice
who can tell the difference
between your voice and mine
rain it's warm like spring
but the black twigs spell out
the real season we talk
it's serious it's someone's life
goddammit tonight at home
high wind tornado watch stay calm

MABLE MCKIBBEN RENSBERGER

grandmother of underground places
your child's hands kept putting flowers out
till every face you knew best was
looking up at you from a clay house

cookie hands garden hands sharp tongue
no more every apron hung up for good every
pair of black shoes that ever stepped over
your grave on the way to another's worn away

from where you look up the sky is deep and
the wind sweeps across the flat acres while
all around you the ones you kept track of
flowerwise are thankful and memorious

EXAMPLES

slipped on the carpet at the turn of the stairs
down! fast surprise — reached out a hand
and did brake myself though the weight of
my body stretched upper arm shoulder and
right side of my chest painfully — but I was safe!

just like a few days later waking too early
in the dark started a fire made coffee read book
waited for early morning news stretched out
on sofa but no luck! nothing made me either
fully awake or tired enough to sleep again
the dawn was delayed stars stayed bright
seemed the sky just got blacker news passed
coffee drunk book still in front of me then
surprise I fell asleep 10 a.m. first nap of the day
so sweet to be unconscious and rest while
everyone else was showing energy scuttling
about at their jobs and making choices and all

or the last couple of days somehow twice it was
appropriate to tell the story about the only thing
about his fatal diagnosis that made my father mad
he'd just bought a new pair of dress shoes
and surprise! you've got liver cancer makes me
so mad I paid ninety dollars for those shoes
and only wore them twice

SURVEYOR'S DREAM

to keep all the directions
in your pocket
to read them in your palm
and sight along the line of trespass

to examine all of this in a mirror
and then decide

to have a lazy man's heart
and feel fallen on by snow
fallen on by wind
to find your footsteps again
by the winter creek

navigating by squirrel nests
to the original monuments
establish the beginning
of the deviation from polaris

to find the order of attention
the order of evidence for boundaries
by averaging errors

to have a directed heart

TRAVEL

atlas of devastation
all the pages blank

thumb through it idly
thinking would I visit this whiteness or that
what would the seacoast look like
empty of sea empty of sand

no need for camera or reservations
pack whatever you wish
no passport no rate of exchange
borders vanish guards and their shack gone

do without a guide
how could he know more than you
how could he be less aimless
impossible to be lost
where all is lost

no one to be a stranger to
yours the only language spoken

endless grieving in an empty place

why worry about heat and thirst
in such a place one has no eyes
no skin no throat to parch

PRACTICE WITH MY EYES

a hero of waiting
whose eyes are medals
awarded for patience

for practice I watch
my breath go in and out
once I almost moved

I caught my breath
with both hands or
did I choke myself

from AMD #6

WHAT FUN IS THIS

the best-tied shoes and most
normal digestion
blackest night for claiming
tire tracks not your own

you stumbled into bed
with the best of them
the covers trampling you like horses

turning away from the door
leaving your house to burn
raise one hand
like a balloon with no thoughts in it
miracle of flame miracle of dawn
that makes a charred wreck of the night

my poor wild mouth
you have galloped through the soup
and (by the back door)
out of the house built for you
by the judgment of generations

alone freezing on the road
the ditches have parasites
the shelters are full of danger

there is no time like the present
and no blackened bones coming up
in your driveway

review
what has been required
and place it beside you like a kitten
later babe later or is it
later even now

SELF PORTRAIT

I am not a poet
hesitating in the shadows of the human door
I am not a poet
for whom the human door has a known handle known
  lock known mat with the key under it
I am not a poet
knocking sentimentally at the human door or in
  another mood trying to force it open
I am not a poet
with his fingers caught in the human door
nor the one
who finding it closed would seek out the mineral
  door instead
I am not a poet
who feels hindered by the human door
I am not a poet
who uses the human door as a coffee table or
  coffin lid

THE MOON'S WHITE BODY

it costs everything
to enter the narrow mouth
of night's one chamber

forsaken beggared
the room's only occupant
speaks the room's only

language a tongue of echoes

YOUTH OF AMERICA

sex now is not the sex it was
in my time sex was held like a day-late event
some of the people who might not have been there
were able to attend
others who wanted to come couldn't

there was a shore
with only a slim strip of sand
a wider belt of green leading up to a stone platform
where the cows were tethered

the clothes we wore didn't flatter us
and what we said was frankly stupid

sex was a boat tied up at the dock of sanity
there was a picnic lunch in it
but the picnic had been cancelled days before
and the lunch was no good

sex had an old dog
I remember this clearly
an old dog who could pick up pennies with his teeth
we liked that part especially
tossing pennies in front of that old dog

the sex of other people
was different but complementary
like two halves of a zipper we always said

in those days we always had sex
instead of a haircut because the barber was lovely

there we were in front of the TV
this was early TV mind you
and sex walked into the room sat down at the piano
and began banging out some damn boogie woogie
    thing
we had to ask it to shut up
the TV was on

where was I
oh yes youth of America
you don't know real sex
sex as it was before you were born
er maybe as it was that caused you to be born
anyway sex was sex was sex was sex was
sex

so if you think you don't have to be grateful
to me or anybody like me
just remember gas was cheap then
we went for a drive
wound up stopping someplace for a hamburger
so I forgot all about you
am I not allowed to forget

EXAMINATION

Called to death's home town to account for the white hairs in my beard, I take note of the orchards in blossom, the full, even stands of wheat, and the one star that broke off from the others to take its place in the netherworld. It is always twilight or just dawning here, the star is alone in a sky of red and deep violet spread like a tent close above. A crowd has gathered at the edge of the hayfield where the dark woods begins. They examine my face thoroughly. My defense claims their sky has too few lights, and the one that is there is cut off from contact with its brothers and sisters. A deep sigh of sympathy runs around the mob. The stars from the other world, it is said on my behalf, have placed the gleams of white (their jewels, their eyes, their memories) to be carried in my beard as a message, knowing I would be called to account and could show my face to the loneliness of the under-horizon with its solitary star. I have nothing to do with this, so the argument runs, and in fact might prefer a black beard or a red beard or no beard at all.

ONE SHELF OF MANY

a book about murdering

a book of lies

a book in which the faces of a history are turned
    from you walking quickly down a side street and
    away from the disastrous confrontation with
    your eyes

a book for the dead to become birds become fish for
    them to stand inside their ribs and look out

a book of children

a book under a book

there are books that have a face and others that
    have legs to run from you

at night you place a book next to you and then close
    your eyes

a book of glass that you see through

a book of beautiful men and their awkwardness

a book that tells you not to sleep

a book lost and then rewritten in the form of memory
    that is of a crumbling wall

this book, that wants to be seen

APRIL

the horizon is only the horizon
if measured from a point inside me

as it looks at me I am its horizon
and it knows its center through my expanse

then there is another point from which is seen
a line between my center and the horizon's

this line is not a new horizon but a verb
beginning an imperative sentence

or perhaps one twig among many branches
that can be seen distantly and will flower

if so I am the bud and must stay warm
and pick my time with care aware of the season

the true shape of the world what is expected
and what surprises remain possible

untitled

it's not possible
he said
for someone like you
to be
well
someone like you

THEFT OF LINES FROM ELIADE, ANGLETON, STOKER, AND ROTHENBERG

Mother of Sleep
who asks us
who scratches questions
on our foreheads

Mother of Sleep
who waits all night if need be
who never tires
it is impossible to say
who or what we are

left to our own
left to the day's
deep devices
we find
the usual inevitables

now
like a road through hills
cuts into us
revealing layers of then

and in his house
of fifty steps
(his house that he gives to us
his steps he helps us take)

killer the golden
studies words
he learned from us
whispers words
he taught himself

HERE WE ARE

the nuthatches land on my porch
weather comes down
the fall it is autumn
autumn is a season of constant veering
the sea lions are barking wait
that is somewhere else
no sea here no lions but there is a barking
I hear at night the house dark
stars send their clear messages
through the trees a neighbor's faint light
yellow answers without speaking
a barking I said that is I know neighbor dogs
but before that a wild crying
could be coyotes who return because
the farms no longer serve to make a living
and the outskirts of town are full of offal
and a tangle of brush in which to hide
or it could be how the sea lions sound
once they've travelled this far inland
lost their way dried out the water saltless
companions buried along the way
one last cry in the moonlight poetic
but obscure since their bodies won't be found
and would be described as something else
since no sea lions here remember
this we know and hold fast to

I WRITE

to tell you how
the loss of your
struck me hard amid my smiles
my blowing kisses to the world
the loss of your

used up my remedies
the usual consolations
are sharp beaks pecking
pecking my most tender

the hills become shadows
my mind moves off among them
my soul left alone refuses thought

those who could help me to
drink to your
are here and there about the world
not gathered nor looking to attend
my hands raised the glass in them
it's no good

my feet are numb
eyes refuse to blink
hair keeps growing
I have spilled

and keep spilling

from AMD #7

FIRST DAY OF SPRING A BLIZZARD VISITS US US

this last snow's weight and power
the piles of it rounding off the flat surfaces the mass
of it bending treetops over till their tips are caught in the drifts
all the early shoots of daffodil and flowers of crocus
hidden under the new shapes discovered in the white folds

our power gone for the lines that carry it
receive their damage too the destruction levied
on all things that have been raised above the earth
the immense silence demanded by so much from the sky
broken as another limb (listen) gets torn from its trunk

for the birds' hunger for their use their mere survival
scatter under the sheltered overhang of the porch
dry seed in quantity on the rare in this white bare ground
where their delicate feet will mark on each other's marks
till there is a printed language of their searching and finding

BOOK OF THE DAY

a version of no corrections

a speech that is perfect with its stammers and running
    out of breath

words like feet that erase and reprint themselves

ink of my eye spine of my joy index of my howlings

the slight marks that cause a change

here on the shelf here on the shelf here on the shelf
    a place to rest

to find a place next to strangers who almost have
    your name

a version of no corrections

NOTES IN HIS OWN HAND
(after Müntzer)

About the destroying condition.

About the surgery that criticizes the condition.

About the vessels, the three girls.

About feeling guilty before leaving the next morning.

About the mother's death; she died destitute, he received
the garment.

About services for hanged thieves sung in the hangman's
church.

About enough to eat, not enough to share.

About giving up prostitution.

About the sequence of tears in the valley.

About the father's death (slow).

About the school and the boy being sold.

About the little brothers' tears, the bitterness of
fosterage.

About the drug that cancels tears.

About the need to expand the hangman's church.

About eating sausages.

About the death of Thomas.

IN PROCESS

giving thanks or sass
having no point and driving it home
forbidding or appealing for help
taking the off ramp from the highway of isolation
singing your heart out (what to do when it's
   emptied)
enlisting confusion in support of clarity
demonstrating the impossible
praying for the unlikely
reminding of the unforgettable
giving up and starting over
repeating inexactly
resisting explanation
stating what can be concluded
ending without a conclusion

CONTINUANCE

a face to look into for
what hides there

eyes like the events of any day
can be recorded so deeply
there is no end to remembering them

what has been lost is concealed
what must be searched for
gains value from being hidden

day rocks into night
night rocks back to day
my grasp is not tight enough
to hold anything worth saving

one thing must substitute for another
and I keep looking in my hand
for the lines I first saw
on another's face

THE AUTOBIOGRAPHY OF
AT LEAST ONE PERSON

a shell game in which
the pea is first smaller then larger
than the hand can move
and wagers are made pointless
by winners forgiving all

for this reason several careers
go off in the wrong direction
difficulties and dissatisfactions preoccupy
the left hand
fails with the zipper

someone sets up a glass jar full of stones
that sits on the shelf till the shelf
falls
wouldn't you know it's dangerous
small dangers large dangers

lightning flashes a tree falls
two are crushed in their tent
but it was a good life they had each other
they acted afraid when they were afraid
and at ease when able to sleep

FOR THOSE LYING WAKEFUL
AS IT STORMS

thunder off in the distance
clear as a closing door
reveals its sad intentions

the night gets a little darker
as a blush climbs its cheek
why recall actions so regretted

and intended anyway only for pleasure
time and shame roll along
together us hiding inside

memory clashes its harsh accuracy
and a moment near satisfaction
shows its backside

untitled

3 a.m. an owl calls out
instead of thunder
a bit of wind crosses the room
and running over the bed
cools me

rain holds off until tomorrow
if I could calm my way
to sleep I would
but every thought agitates

only the owl the wind and me
awake
a few elements make the world
a few elements
and time

THEFT OF LINES FROM CERNUDA

Sleep
is true to us
as shadow flowers
from its object:

a vacant calm
with wings too young for flight
in an isolate dawn
where it hears
no crowing,
nothing.

Desire in sleep goes down
inward corridors
past many cells.
Is it yesterday
held there? Tomorrow?
Neither.

Where the head rests
is a land of exile,
time and history are
banished to the stars,
dormitory of corpses,

and the body has only
its drowsing, the guard it keeps
awaiting true dawn.

10/20/96

my circles run through the woods
sun westers away
as it sets I take my place
on the stone seat by the dry creek bed

gold light gold dry leaves
the wind slacked off
almost to nothing
squirrel's motion cicadas last calls —

three gunshots a pause three more —
this young woods is happy with me here
in the young dark rising out of the ground
all the way through its branches' upper twigs

and on into the seamless sky that soaks up the shadows
and sends back down like a fall of leaves
the night's first images of stars so far off
they have become serene cool familiar

THE FEELING OF IT

North begins hereabouts
its cold lips opening cautiously
its voice telling only
what it is certain of

its long hair catches in the trees
the distances further on and much colder
stretch out a hand

life chores great loneliness
soft eyes hard foreheads
migration and settlement
frost air wonder simple seasons

there is an apple perfectly round
stars forming inside
no emptiness only the feeling of it

TIME TO GO

winter light
roads dim in the fog
trees hold up their evidence
a voice going home
on the gravel lanes led
by deviations written
on the inner bark of sycamores

the crows fly over
they are like us though
their words are higher in the air
and not so easily lost
what happens to a feather
they shed is it drifts
till something catches it
or something else wants
to bear it away

we should get going
the voice will be there before us
we can hold hands
the going will be easier
the chill will leave us

if necessary we can sing
not so far now
pick up your feet
and go singing
the best help is no help
and we struggle so much
our beauty has trouble with us

A PLACE

it closes to them
its narrow pockets
with stern commands

ever almost last
ever sending away its best

in a broad field sky blazes
fertile waters moisten the ambition
of roots to spread widely
the flourishing amazes
those who stand there

experiment of grids
section half section quarter section
on every side the sudden flock
of number

broad field of forgetting of folly
its youth has left and none remain
but those who make a noise
of satisfaction

not calling back nor wanting to
beckon a daring
that would be called great

WHEN I READ

I read to keep steady

I read to gain courage

I read because of my imperfections

I read when loss or fear threaten to overwhelm me

I read out loud I read silently I read without understanding
    any of it

I read as a form of conversation with the dead or distant

when I read my boney hands become artful

like a surgeon's hands they penetrate to the heart of the
    text and close the body up again

in my reading I am not faithless or changeable I am not on
    my guard or hopeless

my legs are not necessary to my reading but they are there
    too

in fact they may have gained more wisdom than my mind
    (see where they have carried me) and more freedom
    than my speech (they offend no one)

I read books newspapers magazines I read boxes menus
    directions price tags I read free offers self justifications
    half truths pleadings attacks confessions diaries

I read pages scraps bridges bathroom walls the bark of
    certain trees dirty cars the steam on mirrors tattoos
    public monuments

I read misdirected mail that comes my way with a thrill that
    at last I will know someone else's truth

I read with my eyes I read with my tongue my ears fingers
    forehead elbows knees

I read the axe's stroke with the back of my neck the epidemic
    with my fevers famine with my hunger

my heart beats I read that my piss is discolored I read that
alone in bed I read the space next to me composed by many
    others
dawn comes I read the sky seasons roll I read the cold and heat
I read with the face of a child hidden behind my face
I am with you now as you read this
we are at the edge of a forest where a plain of grasses
    stretches to the horizon
a river runs nearby we hear its washing everything is breathing
we look in each other's eyes and see the reading
    no I mean we read each other reading each other
when we touch skin reading skin our books fatten until
we are weary and collapse into sleep our dreams reading us
    and what we know so well we have forgotten

from AMD #8

POINT AT WHICH

the speaking of the heart

the point at which it is taken

the door of the house
    its firmness

the movement of the limbs
    their excitement and weariness

the descent of the sky
    it gives everything

the rooftop of the house
    the eyes seek a vision

twelve signs the ear hears
    it is a year that must keep leaving

the speaking of the heart
    its firmness

the speaking of the heart
    its excitement its weariness

the speaking of the heart
    it gives everything

the speaking of the heart
　　it seeks out a vision

the speaking of the heart
　　it must keep leaving

MIDNIGHT

midnight your moonlight
rising back from the snow
on which it fell

your stars and planets
marching a narrow icy path
that goes out and returns

a record so stamped
it can be trusted
even in your lonesome hour —

their faces are shining
though weary
accurate in their eager circuit

their heads bowed to us
their hunger their chill
their fullness whites us all

FOUR BY FOUR

objects I have turned
in my hands a thousand times
their smoke when they burn
carries my sweat away

there the sky was once bare
but now a cloud goes along
a humming rises from my throat
leaving my mouth empty as it goes

water lifts me by undergoing my weight
it helps me to just the height I deserve
like a judge who surrounds with listening
hearing well to decide rightly

last night I was not in pain
stars encircled the house while I slept
I awoke on my knees praying for some reason
explaining my wishes and what I have

1/17/97

the snow blows the road is battered
it hurts your eyes you look down
it is hard to keep going
your feet lift no help
the horizon has fallen open
the wind flies out to swallow everything
your mind is frightened clothes pinch
keep going

PROSE POEM ON THE BAKERS (NO COMMAS)

I always see the bakers when I am in a hurry walking
past the door on the alley where they take their break.
In any reasonably tolerable weather they sit outside the
door on crates or squatting on their heels. Many of
them smoke during their break because they can't do
that inside. I don't think they talk a lot and they seldom
make eye contact with people like me walking past. For
some reason this makes me more aware of my stride
and I can feel it in a way that makes me grateful to the
bakers. They work in a yuppie place that is chaotic and
expensive (a microcosm of our late twentieth century
world) where the customers always seem intent on
their transactions rather than on any personal grief or
joy. I join this atmosphere with enthusiasm since this is
now our way of having a common experience.
Experiencing something in common with other citizens
is sacred or at least has always been thought so. The
bakers in their white t shirts white aprons and small
white caps seem to be (or I would like to see them as)
messengers from another realm of existence whose
message is simply their presence in our world. Hence
their silence. As I walk past them silently my legs in
their regular pace say to me "I get the message I get
the message I get the message."

THE ARGUMENT

A burning house invites the comet in for a meal. The conversation turns ugly and the comet leaves. The house remains behind to see how much of it can burn and it still remains behind. There is a figure creeping near the house, and every so often you can see him look in his hand. He is comparing a photo of the house burning with the house burning. His wife waits in the car. Her friend in the second grade had long red hair and her name was . . . If only she could remember! She would start the car and drive home, her husband would be left standing there stupidly, everything would end satisfactorily. But she will not go until she remembers. The house is very bright now, its flames are waving at the comet, best to let bygones be, no sense holding grudges, especially as the comet is getting ready to leave the solar system. The comet packs its bags with rice and stolen watches, moody. Yes, the house can have its way. No sense stirring up trouble. But it could have worked out differently. Oh well, the comet sighs, I will be back again in some decades, and the house won't even be a patch of black ground by then. Its soot will be forgotten, eyes the smoke made water will have long been dust, but I'll still have my ice and my long hair and my legend.

GUIDE FROM THE PERPLEXED

this is to let you know
there is at least one person in here
frightened drawn out in ecstasy
loved wet loved dry
heartbroken enraged sick all day
trying not to think and thinking
all night helpless with anticipation

privileged to another's body
shaking in his own
capable of anything and trying not to
helpless foolish striking back
lying down standing up
at peace at last or maybe
just exhausted

strain of muscles ache of eye
the hunger need and escape from it
last one left the others gone
beyond recovery and no object
will console no lamb bleats soft
enough not to startle any in this wrecked
home to all who can make do make up

OUR DAYS

my brother in the tree
leaning over our house
sleep that came on us suddenly

there were little terrors
and rainpots in the attic
for the leaking roof

swallows skimming over clover
with their turns and dives and crossings
traced out a name

no a map
to a treasure dug out of our days
of labor and ice cream

no it was a likeness
of my harm effort and laughter
reduced to their strokes in air

that pure art followed
by tidy birds going after
the small lives that jumped from our hay

from AMD #9

WHERE I AM/HAVE BEEN

our decisions are so small
they can be scratched on paper
where my pen touches its shadow
memories crop up
a house ruins itself

I stand at the door and knock
for no reason — no matter how closely
I listen who would say enter

are you with me we are here
or rather on my way
by means of travel whose end
I cannot know

when I began I wanted
to write beautifully
later it mattered less

one thing can be offered for another
ruins for words memory for beauty
trespass for come in

VIEW OF EARTH FROM MY HOUSE

stars out a light breeze
from somewhere passes on

no place is like another
no life has been like mine

night covers morning uncovers
the sun walks like I do

until it can go no further
the seasons walk in a line

patiently with their mass
of changes all around

I live inside them with
freedom and calculation

3/1/98

the sunday walk a path
well trod it is my legs
that made it my stubborn
way of living in the same line
that is drawn out through the woods

creek crossings hard steps
up the hill the earth gives off
a sweet smell like spring
crocus out snowdrops pout on
neck-like stems but trees wait
they wait barely budded
a fine patience to know the season

walking in the creek bottom
a noise from up high
familiar what memory stirs
peering through the feathery sticks
of treetops at the western clouds
the sound comes on what
do I hear I strain to see

then way over the nearest hill
the cranes come clacking
they do not pause they swing north
I wave they do not flatter me
with noticing they travel far
long necks legs wings fly
me admiring the unfaltering journey

REFUSAL TO MAKE MUSIC

I have lost my ears the silence is so large in them

where I am led there will my silence go

my silence won't overwhelm me
it is the rest of me joined to the rest of others
an ocean stretching far from the smashing rocks

full silence has an underlife where I recover my salty nature

where I drown the fish seek out my ribs
I am inhabited by their silence and the little strokes
that move them through my chest

the rest between waves is silent
my heart has a silent moment
if the old hollows of my eyes fill with silence
the tears wash them with a music that does not have to
be made

untitled

sun's careful stroking breaks the frost
worthy effort of the wind to carry moisture
trees swell their buds their eyes open
o urgency that won't rest I give my words to you

untitled

there were some the wind dried some
that sheltered in the curve a tree root made
hanging onto a creek bank some lasted
until it warmed up again some dropped dead
one minute into the new year a path in the brush
a wide concrete highway ocean streams
and channels of air cut through air
carried some to their night rest or day rest
some never moved at all unless something else
moved them some were walking some swam
some flashed through the air some were tired
they lay on their backs if they had backs
some had no eyes to close some lamed themselves
leaping on the rocks there where the ground
suddenly sinks into a cup or funnel some
held out all through the storm and bitter cold
a weather so hard it could break bones if you had them

THINGS THAT ARE AND ARE NOT POEMS

things that kill us

things that we wish were done

things that reveal our better nature

things that with their innocence send up a fresh scent
  from the forest floor's decay

things that are lies

things that fall

things that cower

things that make us smile

things that make us imagine they are something else

things that howl

things that bleed

things that suckle

things that enter us

things that shine and then darken

things that approach

things that can be worshipped without end

things that compel a life of study

things that are cool to the touch

things that vibrate a pathway over our nerves

things that we can know only from memory or
  imagination

things that we resist

things that excite the doctors or make them cry

things that are wrapped around something else

things that overcome us

things that are less than what they were

things that grow and must be cared for

things that have no value

things that we have known since we were children
things that hurt our feet
things that come out of our bodies
things that reflect
things that love
things that arch
things that are the same as other things
things that we will never do
things that stop

untitled

in another dream a pickled man
hands his liver to me
there he says is the grief in the nectar

from AMD #10

untitled

The work defines itself, pulls itself forward, it is
nothing like looking at the work afterward or imagining
it beforehand, it is done with effort, you feel sore
afterward, your mind is involved, it looks on, it goes
into the work and comes back out again to itself, it rests
and something else does the work, the work exists of
itself, it pulls together the place of the work with the
doer, it is neither the place nor the doer, it has left the
doer, the doer is empty of work, the signs of work are
there but not the work, the work is resting in what has
been done, it rests but is still work, the work has no
end, it travels from doer to doer, each of them empty,
none exhausted, the spine is involved, hands, brain,
legs, eye, the parts involved are not the work but only
the means, the work smells like blood, it has motion, it
lives, it is wanted dead or alive, no one has seen the end
of work, it follows imagination, it leads imagination,
the work is not represented by what it does, it seeks
out the doer, the doer sweats, his back will not hold up,
his mind is not large enough, he dies and is replaced,
that will settle him, let him live for that or stake his
reputation on it, he is deserted, he is dust, he lies under
the work, he is silent, the work and the doer: neither
one is sacred, neither one stays the same.

LARRY MILLER

when you call back there to order the flowers
they know how to spell R e n s b e r g e r
but listen politely when out of habit you rattle it off
and Much Love From Your Boyhood Friend
doesn't strike them as oldfashioned sentimental
they'll check about the viewing for you
and manage everything except connecting memory
with knowledge which is left to pain the usual

here's this for Larry: always a fat kid but not soft
deepchested broadshouldered like his fierce St. Bernard
the family business was heavy equipment
backhoes bulldozers and the work they could do
his first vehicle was a red scooter lawnmower engine
pull the cord and go admirable to me the sixth grader
already doing tractor work but allowed only a bicycle
for fun he rode barefoot and used his feet for brakes
even (I saw this) on gravel

last time I saw him was at grandma's house had to be
a decade ago he stood just inside the back door
wouldn't come further because of his muddy clothes
well what I do for fun now is mulepacking I come
down your way every summer go into the Hoosier
National deep as we can get stay there a week so quiet
you don't hear any traffic camp out no work nothing to
do you should come along sometime I'll call you sure
love to sounds great IN MEMORIUM

ADDENDUM TO LARRY MILLER

punched him in the stomach once

high school

it was because he was my friend
never did something like that
to the ones I hated

couldn't really explain it to him after
not sure I said a proper I'm sorry

I'm sorry

THE DROUGHT

if the drought means anything we haven't been told
as a matter of course it seizes our eyes for the water
    they carry
unrecognized by all but a few its mother
    has set out looking for it
she takes no food and rests only when exhausted
the footprints are everywhere the trail is confused
when she asks she is mocked or given useless sympathy
useless because it contains no information other than
    itself
if she hums as she searches her feet tire less quickly
and the marks on her face stay hidden from those she
    mistrusts
when they come out the marks reveal a buried electricity
of which we must be aware and shun as a danger
the long search has made her ruthless and severe
her face is printed in every newspaper as one of the
    ten least-wanted
she believes that somewhere past the dead corn and
    weak flowers
her child has fallen in with dry companions and forgotten
    his home
if only someone would remind him with a few shreds of
    wallpaper
or the smell of the furniture he would be called to his
    senses
and leave his wandering that only brings sorrow and a few
    souvenirs
too delicate for the rough life of no shelving or strongboxes

CAN'T STOP TALKING

sat so still you noticed
I might be thinking and got
quiet yourself till I couldn't
take it and the silence was broke

SETTLEMENT

1.

it is
first the fear of starvation
that makes the town

then the muscles for biting
off pity that strengthen

settlers must be hard of heart
willing to steal their interior

2.

a tide of hands altering the shore

the shore is a line that holds up

who I am is only the outline
of a land where the world arrives

from the loosening shore I am beckoned
to an undefined interior
to shake its mystery into falling

hardship and longing have worn
the trail I follow and drive me
their unrefusing beast forward

3.

in the dark a weariness immune to fear
replaces the blood's rich movement

at the helpless boundary
the body's minerals escape effortlessly
into a landscape without compass

the unmoving place of loss and home

THREE SLEEPS

a sleep that wanders
only as it has always wandered
to the river unafraid of the current
crossing strongly as a question crosses
many answers on its way to satisfaction

one that looks through old photos
of those long ago buried on a hill
to catch when the cold has
locked the ground over them
the snow in drifts that lie on gravebeds
as covers and comforters

the third sleep scolds: three sleeps! where one would do!
its mind is on the insomniacs drifting far out
on their boats of nerves the wind questions ceaselessly
the third sleep knows it would give itself
if it could no matter the distance
would be a rope from the scarred horizon
if rest were a rope

WINTER PRAISES

of abandoned nests
of those whose blood distilled till they disappeared
of cold as a region emptied for the play of survival
of smoke as a shape of various energies vanishing

winter praises snore resting their heads in snowdrifts
everywhere a freedom of blankness
allows feet to mark the earth as if for the first time

(clarity of image parted from object

vacant white as a field for impression a substitute
   memory

hesitations and deviations written out as the exact way
   to follow)

winter praises of mornings tracking lonely after the
   brilliant night
of noontimes' failure and mournful passing
of stars' intensity the greater shining of the darker
   months
of the frost that seals the mouth of every rooted thing
of cold that represents withdrawal and inspires closeness
of the sharp edges of gravel now smoothed with ice

            (I have fallen in the snow and don't mind
            staying a moment on my side
            looking I think like a victim
            stretched on its brilliant altar)   *169*

untitled

what will always be true?
assume you understand that
shrewdness won't help and declarations
must be modified later or abandoned
then it does no good to doubt
love or to grow tired of it

what will always be true?
maybe hunger is a form of love
maybe fear is linked to understanding
knowing hunger fear and the other
urgent shadows thrown by the body
might be honesty if not truth

KEEPING AT IT

I recite the alphabet in the traditional way
walking backwards uphill
with the letters coming out between my feet
one at a time: A B C D and so on

and at the end they begin over again
so it's A one B one and so on
and then A two B two and so on

and so on and so on so on
soon I must get tired the hill keeps rising
under my heels the letters keep appearing
at my toes I recite so well
I can think of other things
such as when will this be over?

and will it end on a Z or
somewhere in the middle like maybe on K
I need to keep my mind occupied
so it won't notice the sore weakness of my legs

but my good heart I can rely on it
it has always a regular beat no matter what
it has opened and closed so often I can think
it will outlast the alphabet S five hundred twelve
T five hundred twelve outlast
the goddamn alphabet

GOLDFINCH ON A WIRE

black line in his feet
various shaded and lit
greens of hundreds of
leaves behind him

his yellow breast
like a child's color
of the sun he doesn't know
how beautiful my eyes

make him the cheer
he makes in me never
enters him if my hand
moves even a little

he flies

SUMMER PRAISES

the ground-filling rain

the rain like spray

the rain driven to violence by the sharp angles of the wind

the strange rain coming briefly while the sun shines

the soft rain yesterday washing into today's brightness

the rain at night that shelters your sleep

the rumbles shouts and split flashes that are rain's
    accompaniment

the rain that digs the dirt and softens it till the sunflowers
    keel over

the rain talking over stones

the gloomy rain that conditions your thoughts

the loving rain the harsh one the one that will not leave

the rain that hides in the cellar or jumps off the roof

the satisfying rain and the one that only teases

the rain in your hand the rain on your shoulders

the rain with a rhythm of blood drowsing you

the rain walking home beside you

the rain apart from you

the rain that never stops singing

the weary rain that wishes to stop

the rain that kills the memory of drought with its own
    green hands

the rain marks in the dust

the rust that remembers rain

the results of rain in tall crops thick air and mosquitos

the rain holding your thoughts in its pocket like a letter

the rain going into your mind through your ears

the delight of rain the boredom of rain the sleepiness of
    rain the rendering of rain as crayola lines
the rain you've grown up with and the new rain about
    to fall
the things touched by rain that are gone when the rain
    comes again
the rain when it was in the clouds was not rain but clouds
the clouds when they visit are not clouds but rain
the rain changes itself and others
the rain dries off the sun is strong you sit under a tree
sheltering as you did from the rain only now from the sun
and the shadows rain down on you

THE STONE BOAT

that sled of thick oak planks
with upturned front we called the stone boat
dragged by a heavy chain through its nose
over the plowed dirt so
we could load it with stones that rose
through the soil each spring
the tractor set to go as slow as it could
sometimes with no driver
and the selection for that field that year
varying: as big as my fist as big as my head

the stone boat loaded full
carried its rock harvest over the waves
of furrows us on top of the heap
or you could say riding its back
dirt as rubbed into our skin
as into the skin of the stones
going to a pile we increased each year
the stones had two weights
one we pulled from the earth
one we lifted to the top of the pile

ONE MOTION

swifts of the city come and go
in one motion

an architect of shadows
in her torn clothes
is building the night sky
while daylight falls to pieces

swifts whirl above
a chimney's mouth
and drop in order down

as if smoke returned
with feathers
to nests not fire

my spirit is in my mouth
where it has been before

where it has been carried
is what I must be able to say

and I find more is true
than not true
and only what can be broken
was ever whole

THE YEAR OF MY ABSENCE

a number of stones under my feet
had faces

the skin of my palms was made of glass

hermits kept crawling out of their caves
holding out their hands
for oreos

this is not what I intended to say
however I must stand by it

and what of the tall bellflower
standing in the garden of speech?
and what of Joe Pye's cure
for yellow fever?

I must endure the indignity of what's said
and with even a dog's luck

I could hang on a little or a lot longer

though it disturbs me that I wake myself
screaming what's my deductible

from AMD #11

WHAT I HEARD

the same sound in the rain coming through the trees
as the cicadas made the day before clinging to them

BECK'S MILL

stands of corn fields of grass and tall flowers
purple white yellow spread up the rounded valley sides
tracts of trees and deeper forest around and no one
looking on from the trees' edge no one sees the labor
in the fields and the workers' slow drag home
no one's hand has drawn up through dirt the stones
that hinder plows and no one hollowed the earth with
    sinkholes
and creased it with creekbeds no one stands in the fine
    night sky
watching the good rest of farms and forest in the cool
    hours
no one has slipped away to the fallen mill's gray boards
broken rooms stacked with moonlight and shadow no
    one's
creaking in the rafters above no one stands nearby
in white light on the grave mound for sorrows without
    name
the exiles ran here and were run again no one followed
    them
no one stayed behind no one is coming up from far away
tonight holding shells sharpened stones and other gifts
that shine in no one's seeing

NEWS

here here here here here
here! here! the jay calls suddenly
from the stub of a branch high up

here what I say it's the side yard
as much side yard as ever
a little soggy this morning
scattered with stript leaves and twigs
grass and weeds shaggy
september sun in patches
but the same yard I always see
the same I stepped on yesterday morning
nothing to see shut up

here! he replies
here last night's wild storm
first fell

TIME RELIGION

worshipped by ticks prayed to
cease by cease up against the tides
up against arthritis we appeal
to next and hang on its saints
the other gods are crows flying in it
water flows through it toxins creep
trees grow and fall wind blows
could it blow outside of time
the wheels under me make hymns
my worship will die
it will be laying with the others
like a plate full of offerings
sins against time are absorbed in the seasons
the morning glory's greed for sun
is checked by frost
sunflowers' proud heads are bent in the direction
their seeds are forced to go
starting each morning with my knees
on calendars I took up the black pen
it was the hand off a clock now the face
is uncertain
we have been living
we will have been living
we will have triumphed over it again
by submission to its sacrament of waiting
there are sanctuaries of forgetting of sleep
of being knocked in the head
we have loved will be loved in it
my hand was on his heart
I could feel the muscle measuring
a time alien to mine

THIS AFTERNOON

I walked over the cemetery
to the oldest part at the back and higher
where the weeds had been knocked down
and the bare fieldstones on the slave graves
looked like shoulder blades sticking up

their names their birth their sorrows
wrongs and work and wonder and words
for it and mouths to speak minds
to call back and look forward
what they built and carried and knew
what was in their pockets or whispered
back at them with a smile before sleep
and their names are in a register closed to me

the stones are sticking up
someone has cut the vines back
and brought down the saplings
sun and shade go by in turns
birds fly over on their way
not far to an unseen shelter
when I hear the cars
over on the road go by
it sounds like someone's life
slowly escaping

TWO BY TWO

in the iron-barred well of a basement window
in an alley one shoe has lurched to rest on litter

the moon out past daybreak seems like others
on their knees and starving

dogs on the road don't mind
they never did mind

I include myself in the traffic moving across the sky
I invite myself to rain down with the others

from thunderheads to ground it's said
if they're in pain their pain can be blown up

MY METHOD

my method
is the residue of other methods

on the open book
notes land
like wasps

they sharpen themselves
against the space around them

my method is to let them
make holes in me

TO THE FALLEN/
IN PRAISE OF FALLING/
THEFT OF LINES FROM TAYLOR

color of flame
rising through trees
the soul rises journeying
flame that escapes us
trees let fall again
the flame that rose
what falls from us
as ashdrift
is love

time falls away
where we cannot reach it
the only thing to do
is to fall after it
ash-eyed you gave
your weight back and
the world taking part
accepted the surrender
as when skies let fall
weeping showers
the ground fills

PERSONAL REVELATIONS OF 2003

I am in my middle errors waiting in line to migrate

the incurable shadow of a dog follows me everywhere

I am fond of migration especially if it involves
    being pardoned and anesthesia

the best anesthesia is of course evening on which
    I spread out my books to relax them

evening is a giant shadow that overwhelms the shadow
    of a dog but it is still incurable

the number of my errors is always half of itself and

the hours I had counted on to move up in line have
    been startled into flight and leave together in a
    flock of one mind glossy in the sun

inside the day given it my life comments on its time

morning (

a ladder of actions

) evening

in my mind I am lying on a beach of pardons listening
    to water yelling for more water and looking at
    an invitation to a reunion of errors

and the return is a long way off from staying put or
    staying apart but I get up and start walking as
    if I were the dog or incurable

THE ROADSIDE MARTYRS

there are no coffins under the crosses they only mark
the intersection where the two friends body and soul
parted ways and made this place the host of the event

bare or studded with glitter leaning over or upright
the colors of their plastic flowers faded in the sun
their home a ditch their companions weeds
the roadside martyrs watch traffic go by with pale eyes

they are counting the numbers for us and remaining
they are the row fate has surveyed by the highway
they offer the meekest of warnings

no miracles are accomplished by them the dead stay dead
the lame limp but we are reminded that no matter how
    lonely
hatefully or carelessly we've lived when the blow falls
strangers crowd around to free us and to lift us away

ENTRY FOR A CHRONICLE

In this year, people's talk was often of peace and war. Great famines and plagues surged across the continents, weather predictions failed, there were reports of murders amongst family members, rebels moved in from the perimeter, signs and wonders abounded. The president sent his generals with troops across the seas and said he would get his man. While all this was happening, certain criminals who had looted billions hung onto their hoard and were still at large. The president's advisors kept mum. The poor were crushed. Distractions multiplexed as people took hope in the refuge of Empire. It was said the price of heroin would go down. A surge of prayers threatened to swamp Heaven, the churches filled again, it was widely said that right would triumph because it was now known everywhere. Things fell from the sky with people in them. In bitter wars far away, inhuman crimes were done in the name of justice, or so we heard. The president was angry at other presidents and condemned them for cowardice or insanity. There were crop failures and starvation. Ignorance was widely spread, and more and more one or another would complain of being ill at ease and unable to sleep. In our own town, the coach was accused of failing, hatred gained strength, it was publicly said the end of time was near. I myself spoke with one who said he had heard voices murmering anxiously from the treetops around the courthouse. And I should report that I was told last summer by a man who has given such things much study that the drought and the oppressive heat had come from our piercing the skies with rockets. The president explained his compassion for those dying overseas and said it made him weep. He offered money, on certain conditions. There were many unusual snows this winter.

MINUS WHATEVER MINUS

sky minus blue earth minus brown
sun minus

white minus crept into the trees
minus bent bough and twig

whatever was standing now standing in minus
whatever minus moves now gone

brother minus sister minus minus me
with you minus my rest

minus my home minus your hands
grip me minus your face touches mine

OUR COURTHOUSE IS BEAUTIFUL

from the southwest corner on a clear April day
the stone steps rising between two old redbuds
their heads bushy with flowers and behind and above
    them
the blocky white courthouse itself backed by blue sky
the lawn is green daffodils surge the larger trees bud out
the monument to all the soldiers and wars is solid
even if some of the lettering is dissolving and the words go

but my favorite monument is on this side screened by shrubs
a tall square pillar with dried up faucets at its base
"drink and be grateful" "thirsty and ye gave me drink"
put up by the WCTU many decades ago in pure idealism
and desire for new laws — did it have a statue on top?
I can look this up — because we are a people of ideals and
    laws

we will break our heads or others' on history if it won't
give way to our banging we have sought a prosperity
to end all prosperity and it never ends the empire
of winners and losers the frontier of it is moving outward
leaving us behind searching the strip malls
for a measure of our limitations

how harsh to love a place that seeks ideal laws
and is always moving away from you
I think it is in a desert now building fires
and spreading ideals our heads have forgotten so sore
from the banging but that's OK I can spin in circles
till I stumble like a drunk in front of the WCTU monument
I can watch the republic dissolve in the distance
into empire and be thankful I'm still here
and lost and ready to fall like a city of millions but really
I'm just a dizzy smalltown provincial who loves April
and stone steps and thinks our courthouse is beautiful

REMINDER

Last summer I looked for the bridge whose enormous
piers cast the swirl of water in the river where Hobie
Johnson drowned. Found a road that dead-ended
between the railroad and the river, a track wandering
through the brush to the muddy bank, a rope hanging
over the water. But the bridge was gone, piers down,
and next day over the river I saw that even the hole in
the mountainside that the bridge led to was sealed up.
The guy who owned a pizza place near where the whole
mighty thing and its traffic of trains had once existed
had saved newspaper articles and pictures of it being
built and later being made to go away. In this part of
the world, everything vanishes without a trace, and then
the without-a-trace is forgotten. Plug a hole, let the frail
paper yellow, words blur, the whole thing gradually
crumbles. True pain and scandal once safely in the past,
we can establish some kind of tourist zone nearby. Put
the graveyard on the hill so the dead get the best view
of the whole thing, while mourners are too distracted
by grief to notice. Maybe some piece of Hobie broke
off, changed form, drifted down the river system —
Ohio in its giant crease between states, juncture with
the Mississippi, Mississippi down to the sea —
experiencing the whole phenomenon of half a continent
emptying itself of rain, dirt, trash, the question of
origins forgotten, that piece of Hobie lost forever in
the Gulf.

from AMD #12

STILL POOL

inked by falling leaves
decomposing in its body

a darkness held
at the ends of branches
all summer

is loosed
beneath the level surface

and the sky
behind the trees
looks up at us

OUR TRIP

it is like
the steps I follow every day
that I haven't taken yet

and the walk along them
feeling I am my own
most desperate reader
the pressure of speech
sailing me through the world

to the mad store
with its walls of words
tumbling around us
its paving of songs and slogans

a ring of fire around the state
the department of the interior
properly erected at last
with bunnies at its corners
to indicate the justice found within

and here is where we sit
the ice cream place
with its excellent beef barbecue

the world of people
is an exchange of light
and shadow
overwhelmed with meaning
I can't say but hope
I have the proper attitude for

ALAN AFTER HE LEFT

missed out on certain sundays
fruit trees blooming like bows tied around the town
news of a crash
chances to feel outrage or sympathy
sunrises with the smoke from houses
indistinguishable from the fog
orchestras and travel and help
a lot of nutty entanglements
grandeur of the hawk lightness of the sparrow
the heart bent by circumstance
trying to straighten itself on its friends
dogs barking horses running

every day he was missed he missed
the center of attention moved elsewhere
or he took it with him like a hat
so huge no one else would wear it
underneath which a song rises in a boy's clear voice
(sunrise after the last hours of night
alone in the barn with the brain tumbling about
memory of the boy's clear voice mixed with the slow light
coming excitement rising with the light the spirit
reckless compassionate attentive
to all listening until the moment comes to speak)

5:55

moon gone
east line not yet even pale
last deepest dark

stars' clear state
the bull's horns high
on the head of night

and at them a meteor flies
its straight trail of sparks
strews fast and flashes out

there or there
a truck growls one birdcall strikes
my neighbor lets out his dog

and the leaves near his house
sound as something small
flushes out of cover

WILDNESS COMES BACK

The wild in America is contained, pushed back,
owned by the people as a public treasure for all time.
Thus it is separated from us and our settlements so
that America can possess its wildness and be free
from it, well-ordered. But the wildness comes back.
In the abandoned pastures and on the rock ledges
made by highway cuts, cedar saplings appear and then
come up in crowds. Along the old fencerows and in
carelessly-tended alleys trash trees — sumac, tree
of heaven — spring out. Scavenger animals multiply,
certain birds find the suburbs and cities to their liking,
cracks in the asphalt or cement breed greenery suppressed
elsewhere, the dumps draw colorful vermin to their
feast. And the wildness takes over new types of habitat,
as when the vines cover abandoned shacks and trailers,
and the rodents shelter there. It takes on new forms
that we don't at first recognize as the wild asserting
itself: toxins and meth labs, birth anomalies and
addictions, unchecked wealth confronted by ever-larger
desires — these are wild, these are crawling over and
under our safe buildings. We are crazy for guns, we
have an insatiable desire for power, control, security.
The law devours wildly, contempt for losers is a wild
passion, money is the wildest thing of all. We make the
largest explosions the world has ever known because
the wildness is in us. We vote for it, we consume it, it
eats away at us, it is the terror our eyes see everywhere,
and we can't stop our hearts beating too fast, our
breath coming out in shouts. We have a wild, violent
desire to get a peace so endless it seems natural to do
anything we can think of to obtain it.

TEACHER

breath of breaths
all things breathing

with this pound of sunlight
and that of dark

the breaking
of breath comes

the fear in high places
comes to lie in the road

daybroken and nightbroken
my heart said teach me

how the grasshopper
lifts his burden

not wearied making of many
duties no end of flesh

and though desire fails
memory also still breath

holds to breath
all things breathing

UNDISTURBED

The night after the poetry reading I slept well but towards morning had a dream in which certain older relations and friends were buried before they were really dead. It's true, they seemed to be dying, but this is murder! I thought, and I felt guilty and fearful of the law, but I admit it was fear of the law that was strongest. But wait, I thought, my siblings helped me and we all agreed, so none of us is likely to report it, and we can still all live easily and long and go to our graves undisturbed by the law.

WAZOO,

out the:
a fullness

beyond plenitude,
comically immense;
as in,

"It was farming country, you know,
hardworking and Protestant
out the wazoo,"

something I said the other day
to explain something about myself.

Numbers don't lie,
we've all heard that,
but they don't communicate experience;

for that, we rely
on bodily events we've all suffered,
something the hearer understands

instantly, ruefully,
and with the humor of fellow-feeling.

Shared experience can
communicate mutual understanding,

mutual understanding
out the wazoo.

ELEGY

told me two weeks before he died
he'd been buying those tennessee tomatoes
from the same family his whole life

started out with the old man
now it's his sons' boys
40 years as a produce man

dealing with them so long was his advantage
they'd always set some aside for him
not wanting to lose a steady customer

WHAT I NOTICED AND WHAT I THOUGHT

I.

trees shook by wind
then still in the calm
by the sound of engine strain
and a random clatter
like hammering
someone up the road
is working

II.

words come
from the world's being
the world presses them
out of us
true though they
wander at times and turn
back on us

but their virtue is
they've grown up straight
in the blowing we give them
and the very sound
of them raises our hearts
our bulwark our guarantee
against wrongs and worries
the violence in the world

man makes and is made of

WHILE THE MASS EXTINCTIONS

went on there were
plenty of places

you would have thought
for all

the dark was dislocated
and room after room

abyss under abyss
(dry for once)

ran away entirely away ran
with the speed light once had

until there was no night either
no hands you might say

could hold up in it
the pulse dispersed

through the fingertips
will be turned back

and buried close to the bone
with its alternate mother

the wind's noise of soothing
and emptying no

LEFT

to have waited
for night to die
and be there
when it's gone
is dawn

EVERYWHERE

this time of year
when brown fields of cornstalks
stand still and night brings
a singing from the woods every tree
carrying part of the chorus
and gardens ache and wilt
overready and tired
walking and walking
I think back to spring
forward to winter
it's not easy to keep my place
on the path for the hardness
that makes it is spread around
the woods and the dead leaves crumbling
and the weeds retired to their roots
open new paths
also the leaves giving up
to drop early set new ways
of sight under the trees
and the track is now no one place
all places equal and the times
that brought us to this and the ones
we approach come together
days of sun and dry weather
the steps to take through them
opening everywhere

FIRST LIGHT

the other great example
like falling into a bath
so large it is not like a bath
at all it is a pond or small lake
the cattails on the slow and mucky sides
and in the center where you've fallen
the depth is part of the water
as struggle is part of the swimming
the depth in a line as straight
as the ocean horizon or
out on the great plains where
heaven and earth express
the even compromise between
their greatnesses by a level at the far
or farthest distance of sight
something out there almost at that distance
leaping and plunging madly
in the tall grass sparked with flowers
just as in former days when
buffalo or call them bison
were a brown flood filling the plains
till they fell in a flood of violence
swept away in that force
still surging about the world
and pulling some down daily
others left to shiver waiting
for the relief workers in their kind boats
balanced on a tide they will not fall into
or we hope they won't fall into
and pray through our eyes holding them up
as they come closer and we weep

from AMD #13

TWO MEN

the man bending over sweeping dust
who could be carrying a hard load
curved as he is by his strict seeking
of those small dull parts

or the one rising from his place
in the tall grass by the river
rousing a dizzy blur of birds upward
mud making his shoes heavy to lift

CERTAINTY

what lies beneath gravity
compelling it
we've never been told

gravity would never say
embarrassed there's a power
greater than it

but we can be certain
it's there
forcing gravity to be gravity

never letting it move
from its center
as certain as we are

the fear of death
makes death be death
and not some flying off

POEM WITH QUESTION MARKS

turn around at the warning sign?

once the perishable road has gone bad?

I have given consent?

making my way downstairs to wait on a bench with the
    others?

remembering the place from which I left?

to match the roads to their destination as the peel can be
    matched to the apple?

to peel it quickly?

form of nourishment: round?

the guest in his room hears the disturbance?

rousing music?

rioters approaching the peak of riot?

survive?

litter?

repair?

picking up from where I left off?

learned men refusing the study of stars?

to chart the wandering ways of men?

setting a banner in the wilderness?

if I were you?

if you were me?

lost in each other's bewilderment?

TO DEAD PLANETS

this cold house
some amongst us
disinhabittedly
share burnt and
poisoned stones

LATE WINTER

my stiff legs on these winter stairs
scoured by orbits the realm shines raw
the new moon is bent against the dark
in every house a fire is burning

what a pile of ashes I make!
and eat oranges

SOME EVENTS

some flakes on the way down stopped by
and therefore piled up along the fine branches
outline the lacing of the woods running
up and down the hills and into the ravines

the square empty shell of the grist mill's
foundation walls opens to the clear or greenish
water of raccoon creek that rose and twice killed
the mill till the old man wouldn't rebuild
but wouldn't leave the land either
so he lived on it till he died and left that way

if you park by the stone angel in the corner
of the cemetery the walk on the muddy old road
over to the track going down and across the face
of the bluff under the hemlocks then creekside
to the ruins takes twenty minutes

ITS FIELDS

green wing of the hill
a world in flight
the creek's hands working all day
on the stones' tumble singing

the knock at dawn
woodpecker working overhead
hunger lifts him there

and the young tree which storms
shook shaking
with new leaves broken out
broken at her feet the body
feasted on the heart torn
open when the talons pulled

air layered light and heavy
storms from the heights whirling
lightning from dark nests
flies singing

a night coming full
of shaking and singing
a night drawn over us
deep in us working all
through our sleep and breaking open
its fields of us

IF GOD IS LOVE

and love is a consuming force
that empties us

breath stolen for sighs
lonely hollow deep

eyes staring
abstract organs of devotion

heart burnt into heart
till neither moves without the other

love the binder and love the breaker
setting up against order desire

then

ONCE AND AGAIN

the statues are not statues
but the temporary conspiracy
of stone and mind
broken by the sun's investigations

see how they fall apart again
unable to agree
you look at it once it's all stone
look again all mind

THERE

in that place
where we put windows
there are mirrors

where here
a mirror would hang
there is a window

when you
look outside
you see inside

when you wish to
see yourself
you are shown the world

from AMD #14

SOME MILLERSBURG

of your own
not mine

its streets end in fireflies

a crown of corn around it

trains pass nightward clanking
under the electric cross
erected over the grain elevator

it has its own sky
arching bridgelike above

fish fries and the singing

BLACK AND GREEN

on state road four you came down
off the little rise curving
into the flat stretch at the bottom

black dirt one big field
each side of the road
green rows fat low

dirt deep as time
the mintiness of the muck land
in the early heat

one morning has other mornings inside it
one life has time in it it fed on
till scented and green from the feeding

GROCERIES

when you think you see
a dead man in the cereal aisle
and then realize it must be someone else

it's not true

the dead come back so easily
we mistake them for our own kind

the lack of recognition does not insult them
they remember how easy it was to assume
life and death are separate things
and anyway

they are busy looking for something
in all the choices we have laid out for ourselves
so caught up in the search

they barely notice us
till later when they think
oh wait that was him
he must still be amongst the living

SEPTEMBER, 2005

huddled masses

untitled

I kept a
list of words
used only once
until I saw
I was using
them again and
it was no
list of words
used only once

THE MIDDLE OF MY LIFE

when I reached the middle of my life
I paused

clouds flew like flags overhead

a dog raised its head from sleep

there was something bothering me
something was happening but I couldn't
   put my finger on it

I thought awhile

a bird gave a triumphant whistle

the air was momentarily moister

a car went by

later I would realize that it was at this
   moment that hope diverged from fate
   and they went their separate ways

but the moment of realization also
   passed without my noticing it

I was busy realizing and the moment got
   no attention

I speculate now that there was the sound
      of running water in the distance

also a cricket vibrated its drumsticks

a leaf flashed briefly in the sun

a squirrel on a nearby branch looked at a
      nut sighing

then it was over

THEFT OF LINES FROM KHLEBNIKOV

the gouges in the sides
of a tree a hill
gouges on the surface of the river

the larger birds we see
travelling some of the longer distances
Péeoo! Péeoo! pyak, pyak, pyak!
drag their legs behind useless
while they rely on their spread wings' power

having opened with a surge of light
the day closes its statement
moving dullwards under blob clouds

when the root stirs
the old stem breaks at its base
Ek, ak, oook!
it has blown up the history of last season
taking sides in the contest of
memory and experience

WRITING AT NIGHT

its chief object
like shouting at the deaf
clarity

between the tweakings
and so on of the birds
close examination

of your emptiness
which it turns out
is an illusion

not emptiness after all
merely rest
but not undisturbed rest

NOSTALGIA

the rain is an empty city
each drop a building evacuated
its stairways uninhabited by echoes its doors and windows
useless for keeping anything out or in

each as it falls standing in relation to other drops nearby
each one composed as if it were thought of only by itself
or perhaps designed with just its near neighbors in mind
but the many drops crowded together form a gigantic
        pattern
as though this pattern as a whole was foreseen and enacted
but each drop knows only those near it
and nothing lives in any of them

the rooms are empty the roofs are empty the streets and
        squares
hold no one and there is no one in a hurry or with time
        on his hands
there are no glances no quiet agreements to slip away
        together
no first disturbing signs of an illness no firm deals made
no great bargains or agreements to buy later
no betrayals or bitter arguments between old friends
no one is there to love or to lean against when one is
        tired of all the activity of the day

in fact one is not there oneself one has been emptied as
        the city has been emptied
as if one had never existed as if no as if that included
        the hypothetical possibility of one's imagined existence
        or extinction had ever been uttered

as if the one certainty left is a zero in place of an I

and in such a city whose citizens have reached such a peak
of non-existence

the streets broaden a little new buildings are not constructed
old ones fall

through the wider spaces between what still stands a fresh
wind is blowing

it parts the buildings or we should be honest the raindrops
further

the sun comes down these channels like an ancient triumph

the onlookers crowd closer to see the chained slaves and
elephants

the sun is filling all the space now

one can only feel nostalgia for the stark uninhabitation one
has lost

standing there thinking of it crowded by the sun and all those

who go by never having even heard of the empty city

SELF-PORTRAIT (WITHOUT MY FACE)

ambivalent about irony
always a little sorry

occupying the place
where sorrow and joy
by aligning eclipse

the lines drawn from one loss
to another touch and depart
a web cast everywhere
with a tug at the center

walking along the stone wall
the storm moving off among the mountains
the lone center of the great field
millions of grasses acres wide
some striking wet at my knees

FIVE THOUGHTS BEFORE SLEEP

the sand the shore moved
so many nights drifted together

out of the sun's hive bees of light
give as to their keepers
honey without stings

I might have been there too
with myself that lonely day
before I had this thought

I have never done anything
but dream what I do

the night distances
scars shimmer overhead
the ancients in their wounded state
appear

WE KNOW THIS

The dead are sleepless, we know this, they need no rest.
With no sleep comes no dreams, and they live in reality.
Unlike us their reasoning is perfect, they accept no
delusions. Like the ants their nation is rational, unerring.
They cannot be hurt: no fear. Numerous as they are, the
way they live ensures that their needs do not empty their
surroundings or crowd each other out. Wakeful, reasonable,
faultless, desiring nothing and never afraid, how could we
ever understand them even enough to be enemies? Surely
they must be puzzled by us, too, since the only thing they
have forgotten is the need to sleep. They must wonder
a little, if they ever notice it, how still we are hours at a
stretch, eyes closed; never guessing at the impossible
things we live through every night.

from AMD #15

LATE SUMMER BEES

a creek of broken stones
when the weather dries

the bees' last hunt
for anything sweet before frost
urgent buzzing angry

and from the branches above
a clash of hard voices from black beaks

surrounding it all
the round land repeats itself

the shape of the creek's emptiness
is a memory of water

and we stopping here a moment
remember a silence that once
covered the breaking in us

A THEORY OF LINES

wind bent by the objects it surrounds

comfortable by the grave of empty space

each one admits something the others don't

said another way none can contain it all

from before dawn till deep dark I run a line through
     one day

my voice is a thread that goes only so far before breaking

the earth's slow curve is expressed on the great plains
     by a flat line of horizon

in cities buried unknown beneath mounds lines still
     living were first spoken

the lines come out of order and I try to straighten them

my failings and furies will end and the lines remain

jettrails mark the sky the page fills with lines and so on

and

LAST CRICKET

in the hickory's crown
a host of yellow has settled
endless time has entered the room
not all lanes remain open
the way I must go is set

the cricket in his bed of leaves
soothes one's loneliness a bit
as he did all summer
I wait in the still dark
one sound and then another

untitled

a cold rain
I can see the darkness
just outside my windows
but not the deeper night beyond

listening to the drops
scatter themselves on my walls
I look into
the whole dark of the world
almost as close now
as my own face

and think of you
it is as though all the dark
and you look back

HIDDEN BEHIND BELOW

the courthouse square almost empty
but for sparrows and that shadow
at the shrubs' feet that just now
twitched deeper into the tangled stems

the thought that is the grandparent
to your thought remains in the world
though its stillness makes it
undetectable
all the midnights of the years
will crowd around the next twelve struck
you are not the same
though from moment to moment
you think you are

hidden behind below
is another depth so weighted
with all the nows that
everything blurs in it

and its density of experience
harder than what made it
becomes another experience

SEVEN DEER

earth in your determined ring
you pass between fire
and boundless night

into which bright stars
fall deeper distant
days becoming more distant

on your back a slick of life
from which grow two flowers
mystery and reason

you sent from the low woods
walking east across my drive
seven deer in the young morning

so much the color of the woods
and the gray damp day
they would have vanished

once back amongst the trees
on the other side except
they move they move

DREADNIGHT

those few still awake are hidden
from sleep and won't obey it

they have
hands with grass-like changes
shake of the wind blown through

the constellations rise and set
the housebeams tick

time does not pass
it only disappears

and they are left holding
the traps they hoped to throw on it

MY CONDITION

the small white moths
which flapped ankle height
away from me over the litter
of the forest floor
were carrying on their backs
the seeds of the night

night has grown so tall
it covers my condition
with its thick spray of space
and one moth that escaped
followed me here to test
between the lamp and my face
for where it will rest

WORLD IN LOVE WITH ITSELF

all motion is one motion
see the astonishing
boundary light and liquid
have made for themselves
how flight is an element
those plain dark birds have found
how the black caverns throw
themselves crookedly into earth
and the air over soil makes
itself too green to see through

PRAYER

we thank you for all the justice that is in the world
for the compassion mercy love people show each other
and for health long life plentiful food quiet streets
spacious living rooms we are profoundly grateful

our peaceful neighborhoods mainly loveable children
moments of relaxation relatively small payments
variety of entertainment quick access to help
(emergency!) power given to see all ease of travel
sound sleep at night wealth of supplies lucky friends
freedom from confinement harsh guards illness boredom
long hours of terror brutal labor pain of memory pain
of anticipation heart closed inside itself from fear
all move us to joyous and frequent thanksgiving

and that the frequency of thanking has become
so repetitive that we can do it without straining
a gesture as well learned and casual as setting down
a cup without spilling yes for the very unexceptional
and almost thoughtless gratitude we are able to have
for this above all we shout rejoices and praises
till the noise of it rolls away distant and harmless
amen

TO A BUZZARD

cousin
what solitudes you invent
with your brethren
circle on circle
just under the sun

silent as breath
your breast a midnight
your wings the sails of midday
dire hour of maximum light
you cruise the open sky
over the sagging earth

where your dark roost
is hidden you will fold yourself
after the day's sailing for study
of what the stars' vaster circles
can teach — their helpless heights
and far more brilliant solitudes

PERSEPHONE

amongst the dark columns
where she lives forgetting
is best to ease the gloom

but a bee hived in her heart
will not stop buzzing over
last year's heavy sprays

and her heart moves thick
in memory no matter
how commanded won't mind

MILK BEER WATER

in the beginning it was milk milk milk
all day long

later it was beer beer beer
like it was milk

then water water water
the cleansing liquid

now it's milk beer water
in moderate rotation

oh wait
don't forget the coffee

WHO MADE IT

if I am in my labors
I can only really be seen
in what has been done
through them

we at this table
are seated where he
who made it made
a place for us

and when we speak
across it the words are
an opening where the ghost
of his ghost stands

from AMD #16

AGREEMENT

The cabdriver walking home from his shift said, "How ya doin?" as I pulled the newspaper out of the coinbox. Pretty good, I said, but it could be a little warmer. Don't want to wish too hard, though, or it will turn a hundred on us. "That's what we're like, isn't it?" he replied. "Nothing makes us happy." We laughed in agreement. It was funny to both of us that nothing makes us happy.

THE POEM

I was thinking standing at the top of the hill
of the poem that could be written from there
that could have its place there or
I mean be one of the things unique to that place
a poem that could not be removed
not because it would die but
because it could exist nowhere else
and if moved would then exist nowhere
a poem of and only of the hilltop
not this one

LIVING THINGS GIVE BACK WHAT
THEY GATHER

grassy field seen through the tree stems
and the muffling of the fog shining back
the sun's purity of heart from every tip
end and blade edge into one glory lights
with reflection the haze shrouding us in

FIRE

when and if the sparks
flying land a conflagration
starts and the smoke raised
shades the light bursting
from the fuel's body

the edge of fire splits
into things where they join
and from the opening there
comes mutter and shout as
air moves from the energy
blown through it a stir
so brief it can't be saved

USEFUL

the tremor is useful for mixing things
in a cup for brushing specks away
for surprising myself

in the midst of writing with new forms
of familiar letters

they take a shape as unintended
as what is said can be other
than what I tried to say

in this way it is as if
I am being talked to or receive a letter

so exciting I open it with shaking hands

ACCEPTS

summer comes to rest
in a room of shriveled objects
underneath each leaf
a silence clings
overhead the blue flame
of the sky reaches up
earth has set its dry lips
in the form of rivers
to catch the nearest rain

everything now obeys its needs
in order to manifest its true being
the well for instance
must have depth
to truly be a well
and to have the depth
it accepts in its water
a grit flaked off
the ancient stone
through which
its needs drove it

untitled

the rush of air overhead as I sleep
no one speaking to no one listening

ME WALKING IN NATURE

Looking in all directions, no one to be seen: I am
alone. Here in the woods, I am a minute speck of the
upthrust, the wave of human history. A grain of dust,
a drop of spray, a bubble. I am closer to the infinitesimal
than to the infinite. The exact particular that is me
stands here amongst those not of its kind carrying
within it the species. Nations and tribes and solitaries
who all knew their something represented here by me.
My nature is us, having come off the savannahs and
wandered, not a quest but a question: what is over
there? This leading not to an answer but to a result,
which is me standing here, looking around, probably
looking a little daft, if truth be said, to someone
witnessing, if a witness were to be found, which is not
found, but nonetheless there it is, the person standing
by himself who could not be there if others had not
moved before, would not be dressed if others had
not clothed themselves, would not even have a thought
but for the thinking together built all through time,
and therefore, truly: he is not alone.

WRITING WITH THE COLD HAND

a couple of pages back:
winter's teeth
the face of the north
we descend solemnly
to year's end

a couple of pages ahead:
the white still slumbers

music always passes on
to where it is barely heard
and then to where
it is no music at all
I listen into it
for the bite of silence
where it begins

SOMEONE WHISPERS IN THE EMPEROR'S EAR

and he knows what to say next
his commands are his obedience

fact and the laws dependent on facts
one the crown one the interior
of the crown he wears
the circle it constitutes constitutes him

he is nothing but a word
that refers to a realm
so large the last village
has forgotten the first

where an openness to settling
new borders dissolves all borders

THEFT OF A LINE FROM MERWIN

that hand moving a touch towards me
I can never outrun or return

that voice following me
room after room asking how shall I live

the storms I've lived under
the clocks repeating themselves
five five five or some other number

the complete fire
I know my world is making
and the liquid caught from its alterations

account for only a measure
of what was lived

from AMD #17

untitled

the stone says
I dealt the blow
pick me up again
there is a use
I have in your hand
neither the hand
nor I have
in ourselves

8/25/09

it was hot like this
my first day too
chickens expired in their coop
people consoled themselves
with the thought of september
the clouds which refused us rain
were said to be the most beautiful of the summer
as they sailed by

I couldn't put anything into words
I was all about sensation
and flapping my arms around
having no place to keep memories
I was likely to forget the day
as soon as it happened
nor could I look ahead and imagine
that tomorrow would be a better day
or a worse one
no one could teach me a thing

probably I cried wholeheartedly
and ate and shat and slept
the sleep would have been
the same as waking
no difference between
things I dreamed
and things I saw
all unformed too new to be bizarre

there! I would have said to myself
if I had had speech or a self
to speak to
that's number one and now
on to number two or whatever it is that's next

AUTOBIOGRAPHY VOL. IV

we had been told many things
but we had never heard of the world
so we were unlikely to go there
or complain about its circumstances

after being told there was nothing else
and nowhere else to go
it was all we could speak of

smoke drifting around many houses
smoke rising from one house alone
rain tilted against my face
the wind sharpened itself on the plains
and dragged the cold over to us

at night my eye went from light to light
all the way to the edge
stories gathered around each of us
all were warmed
all listened

the smoke could only go
a short ways from the house
before it fell apart
or you could say
the world and years
gathered it into them

LOOKING AT A FLY

how far back to our common ancestor?
some swamp the ferns thick in the heavy soil
orchids dangling from some gingko or gymnosperm
poking around in the moist slop for something to eat
sex perhaps a new thing just a compulsion not enough
neural action yet for it to be an interest or make society
the common trait surviving in us both would be curiosity
a what's that? response but on the level of voluntary motion
not any kind of true awareness as either you or I know it
fly I salute you as my brother or sister can't tell which
do you like me notice we share the feature of a face
I rub my hands together too keep your feet off my food

LISTEN LEARN

the flames flying
by night
have heard the stellar fires
say come quickly

the drops of water
are a school
for learning oceans

and I

I

a drop of water
a flame

ROUTINE

Every morning, coming out of sleep into the stark surprise
of day, having roamed all night outside of myself in the
empty familiarity of dreams, I must put my self back into
myself. Before I get out of bed, almost before I blink my
eyes. There is a moment at first light, as I am about to do
this, poised between an emptiness and the not-yet-full,
when I am no one. In these few seconds, no one has his
entire day.

no one opens his eyes and listens
no one stumbles downstairs
no one takes in the news
no one eats when he is hungry
this will be repeated throughout the day
no one cleans himself and heads to work
no one works
no one works till after dark
no one goes home tired
no one passes the time for a few hours
a friend of no one calls sometimes
no one has his accomplishments of the day to recall
no one is ready for bed
no one sleeps and may or may not dream
and if he does dream may or may not remember
no one's body stirs as the night pales away
no one is willing to wake
no one must become himself again
but for a moment before he does
no one is no one

THEFT OF A LINE FROM WHITMAN:
THIS WINTER

five thousand games of solitaire

snow repeat snow

touching my face with stiff fingers

extension of immensities

everything is lost in everything else

dry breath

when I can't travel I call it a break in my plans

when I look for the marks of this winter

I find a shower of white sparks

everywhere between my hat and boots

ONE BY ONE

inamorata
my bride of the woods
the world is too big to know
I feel weak
as you do in a dream
when you want to run

camerado
in the flats where
we have lain
our imprint is gone from view
it is a secret knowledge pressed
into the roots of the grasses

little self
wandering in the forest
of my body
you hear the memories
call to you from
just out of sight

over here! over here!
you are not lost so long
as you know how
to follow forward and your steps
in case you need them are
still there for backing out

ALL SOLITUDES ARE THE SAME

All the solitudes. Each keeps to itself. Happy hours.
One speaks at last, to be known. Then he's dead. "He's
only playing dead," another solitude says. "Just like him."
The solitudes closest by move closer, to comfort.
Nothing. As if their words were unheard.

STONECRUSHER

I went back to the roads I grew up on and walked daily
there was one I used to take to my grandparents' farmstead

it was made of concrete by the men of the neighborhood
in the thirties to give them work to earn a bit of cash
they told me a stonecrusher had been brought in for the job

I could imagine its massive metal parts and power
and see the scoop taken from one side of a little rise
just off the road where rocks were found to feed its appetite
I knew by the trees that filled the dig how much time had
    passed

it was snowy back there half a year ago when I made
my return and now here today it will get to ninety
the sun coming through the wet air presses a weight on me
and I am writing down my recall of the trip I made
to record how I remembered my grandparents' stories

SO FAR AS I CAN AGAIN

the trees at night stretch out
amid voices croakish old
in a dark shared with white eyes overhead

between banks of sunset sunrise
a river of shadow cuts its way
wherever it can press its claims

to be trusted with the gold rise
of the moon and me as I am
empty I am light enough

to be carried away easily on it
at rest on a bed of reflections
from houses backed to the river

I eric rensberger poet
of these words run them again on
my tongue smooth as night runs

between day and day
these reflections of my days grow longer
and still I have

so far to go again
I share these reflections so far as I can
for I have the hands and mind for it

wind is up cooler now the eyes fly on
some have gone the easy dark holds me up
and I could almost say I've arrived

AUTOBIOGRAPHY VOL. V

I disappeared
into the world

one of the creatures there
the clocks began counting me too
with the hours I fell into

my direction slanted with the wind
the world's sight came through my eyes
now for the first time ever
my point of view was included

what a difference!
I would never have recognized
a world that didn't contain it
and it has been my distinction
to be that view the world holds

IT WILL WAKE

the drunken species
unable to protect itself
too loud too unsteady
dancing fighting kissing crashing
so sorry it can't stop crying
so happy it can only expect more
surrounded by accidents
every sentence it starts ends in confusion
lovable meanspirited lost
looking for the key pissing its bed
a slap a tumult the sway
as helpless as it is dangerous
can't tell it no can't stop worrying about it
sad really a threat only to itself
but no — reckless friend of death
when passed out the worry is it will wake

from AMD #18

THE DREAM OF LAST NIGHT

dreamt of rain

60 plus a week

the rich sound of it inside me
all my ifs and whens burst into now
but a conditional now

the condition of dreams
where the rain falls
but doesn't nurture

dry skin and wet inside

60 plus a week and a night

morning takes away night
nothing takes away dreams
they linger in daylight

the memory of the sound of rain
in a dream is worth as much
as the memory of the sound
of rain in daylight

LAST DAYS OF SUMMER

the long dry spell weakens everything
leaves hang on a thread
I am pulled out of sleep
when my breath catches in my throat
the seasons pass into each other
without a welcome with nothing to show
for all that time spent waiting in the sun
somehow enough survives to bite me
when I walk through the brown grass
and at night through the open window
the chir and hum and croak
also somehow survives

A MAN

as I left there stood a man
staring at the street I was about to cross
his hands in his pockets
his clothes neither good nor bad
hair thin back straight no one standing near
he was not waiting for anyone
he had nothing left to do
nowhere to go
and in truth nothing to look for
out there
where he seemed to be staring
when I glanced his way
as I stepped out to cross the street

A SQUIRREL MAKES A MEAL OF ACORNS

it looks up and sees
an edge of the sun
come over the edge of the earth

someone is writing down
observations of this
filling page after page

note number one:
the occurrence of anything
ruins a possibility

number two:
after it's over
there will be time to think

three:
big sun little acorn
hungry squirrel curious man

THE DIVER

the tomb lid sketch a naked man his body arched
to curve against the arc his fall accomplishes
they say it is an image of an old belief
life is one long fall death a gravity
the wise make beautiful yielding as if willing
here the body's weight is image of soul's fate
and life an action only partly willed an arc
that anchors in a swell of wine-dark mystery

was he who lay beneath the slab as beautiful
as that diver or was he simply rich enough
to be depicted so? I hope they paid him well
the one who painted it I mean for we who stare
upon it now can give him nothing but our late
appreciation useless as it is to him

NEWS

somewhere peace has begun
the real the permanent peace
the people love each other
all work is respected
no one has to fend for himself
justice can be had for just the seeking
and all agree it is fairly given

but we don't know where this happened —
a small place off the maps and
from the satellites all that can be seen
is the green fur of the heads of trees
moreover they too have forgotten
the way to us
we have become only a theory
or a record of someone's memory
of what he was told as a child
by an old man whose name is now lost

IN THE HIERARCHY OF POETS

I attempt to find my place
this branch is too narrow

on that one they never stop arguing
and always I am jostled
by those who wrote long before

how annoying to be pushed by a corpse
this one belonged to he
who stole writing from the accountants
he justified himself by saying

I have a better use for it
but he never proved it
thievish stinking gabby old man
who lived so long
he forgot his own name

ERIC RENSBERGER

The date and cause of his death are unknown to the present writer. Serious discussion of these matters could boil over into obsessive contention. For this reason, I must declare that they do not affect the concerns I address here in this particular work. While I fully understand the importance this subject might have to some, nonetheless I must refuse to diverge into it, for no benefit can come from such speculation to this writer or to his work.

HERE

Here where the alleys cross all the ground has been
asphalted over for parking behind the houses that have
become businesses. This used to be where children
played, the plot of vegetables was laid out, backyard
chickens scratched. The twenties, perhaps. "Ja-Da"
reproduced phonographically floated outside through
the screen. And earlier? Horse hoof clops, buoyant
confidence of the Christians, class contention, the rail
lines coming to the center of town. Before that, grieving
over the Civil War that had been cheered forward from
all the porches around, soldiers parading away. And even
before, taking over from those who had been marched
out of sight, saving an occasional thought such as Indian
Creek for them, otherwise refusing to remember. And
then those long millennia backward we scarcely hope to
know, the time before men when a shaggy beast pressed
a hoof here or a dragon strode. The time this spot lay
under the sea accumulating a fine dust of tiny bodies
into mud and then rock. And this spot was here when
it was all hot gasses or a space of nothing, this spot
here where the alleys cross.

OF STONE, STONE

to speak of stone
stone is the word
to use

to speak of stone
at a distance
say mountain
or world

to speak of stone
intimately
say bones
are made of
broken minerals

MY FATHER'S GRADUATION PORTRAIT

your youth faded far more swiftly
than this image of it
whose smile still leans out into the world
and whose eyes though they have never seen anything
seem to touch everything

the image fades only slowly
and retains to the last its initial form
and then? it is nothing it has done nothing
but hang on to a trivial moment of your life
when the photographer called for your attention
and a smile

this image is nothing and engendered nothing
because it did not depend on the continuance of a
    heartbeat
it only needed itself and some stiff paper
and therefore it outlasted you and came
into these days of mine which are almost as many
as you ever had
came into these days and before my eyes
which really look really see
not like those eyes of the image
dead from the moment the shutter closed

HOPE

Never easy in his mind, that man still keeps hoping. It's
true: the great keep wealth and power to themselves,
liars prosper because we love to hear a lie, each of us
who fears another is feared by someone else, and we're
all absolutely right to fear: none is trustworthy. "So what
is there to hope for?" That's not the point. Justice,
kindness, and peace of mind are meant for the realm
of imagination, not for here. There, all sleep is pure
and beautiful, the days are harmonious and even-paced.
We would not fit in. The animals of that place would
attack us as strangers who do not know how to treat
them. We are of this place, that always breeds some
"next" from its "before." A tree whose roots fail and
branches fall is drilled with holes, some featheration
gets busy there, coos its tune from the opening, eggs
are begun. When one shade is struck down, the sunlight
falling on the earth draws up another out of the seedlings.
It's not so much that in this place everything exists in
time, it's that time is in us, all of us, trees and rocks and
airs included. That man never easy in his mind doesn't
really hope for help coming from the hills or plains,
seas or mountains — what he calls "hope" is time
moving through him and leaving a trace he can feel and
must embody in an image of what has not yet come.

from AMD #19

HIS EYES

Grant shades his eyes. He can see what could happen. He knows that others can't see what he does. He looks into the future — not the distant future, years which contain things which would astound or mortify him; the future he sees is only a few hours away, and isn't even a future but merely a possibility. What the men could do, what would happen to them. At any rate, he knows he cannot describe the exact vision to his subordinates — it would confound them, and take too long to explain. Grant shades his eyes and looks for a few simple things that can be described in plain language. The others look to him for their orders. He is looking out over the landscape to see the words he will write down a few minutes from now.

AT THE SOUTH UNION CEMETERY

my shadow entangled with the other shadows

the facts of what occurred lie all around

stones in rows surrounded by corn in rows

a complete demonstration of ripening and its results

there was a word spoken here a half century ago

it sank into the earth with the rest

its message lies there with the rest

my message to the future is

we did what you demanded of us
and we know the demand was not yours
it was imposed by some further off future
also beyond our reach

to be born amongst the billions is to spit into the lake
every breath taken must be given back again

night is shadow laid on shadow
and it has no opposite no time without shadows
at exactest noon there are shadows under our feet

my message is

we have forgiven you in advance
for if we condemned you we would have to
blame ourselves for the past

GINSENG

a pair of golden hands
holds up a bundle of polished red stones

if some trespasser comes
to dig the root

I will never see those hands again
so I take the ginseng myself

and move it to a bed
in the shade near the house

prepared as the books say to do
with rotted leaves

the root in my hand looks like
a plump little man

so fast asleep
his limbs dangle from him

and the stalk and leaves
are like a dream rising from his head

that night I again dream I am a thief
I escape safely

with the gold in my hand
across the dark plain

to a range of nought where
nothing pursues

where there is
no dream no dreamer

a sleep that has been emptied
even of anyone to say the word sleep

MY PRIZES MY AWARDS MY HONORS

that reading those decades ago
after which an old woman came up to me
and said she was glad my poems had silos in them
young people need to write poems
with silos in them

to my horror Dad told me he'd shown
the poem about an older relative
that detailed the comical scandal of his life
to my cousin the man's daughter
but then he told me it made her laugh
that she loved it because she had loved him

that younger poet who corrected me
when I complained that the only thing
people in town remembered me for was a poem I wrote
quickly and mostly for amusement twenty years before:
"it's an honor that they should still like it"

me, ashamed: "of course you're right"

WHAT OTHERS THINK

no longer matters
the debts you had
will be covered as if
you covered them yourself

did it ever matter?
how can the thoughts
of others be known?
it all went out

of the world instantly
your thoughts and theirs
the stories of course
still hang there

in the world attached
in some way to it
though how this is done
I can't be sure

3x5 SNAPSHOT

Five Buzzards on the lawn, all related to me. The black
clothing of the one in the middle hides all but her
inscrutable face. Salome. Of the men, one is Doc, one
is Alpha, one is John, one is Moses, who made popcorn
for his people on the square in Wakarusa every Saturday.
The town band playing, farmers selling from their
wagons, children running screaming to and from the
store with the soda fountain in back. It is full summer.
A tree massy with leaves towers behind them, a dirt
road runs nearby with more trees behind it thick enough
to close off the horizon. The grass is worn where they
stand, and there is a low white railing marking the edge
of something — a parking area? a field where children
play? a lot deeded to a church for a graveyard? It is a
summer day. The weather is fine. They have survived
one century and stand sturdily in the next. They are
there on another day of the absence of those many
who were old when they were young and tried to
explain the exact mix of sternness and gentleness
necessary for life. It is only a photograph, not reality,
the present moment. But they know that, photography
or not, any moment of the moments we've had can
come back, that they all continue just because they once
were, even if the snapshot is lost, the people long gone,
no one to remember, no story to tell.

TO PASS THE TIME

I thought of pretending it was 35 years ago but I couldn't

the light of that year is 35 light years away now

the happiness and unhappiness of it have been stirred
together

the dead of that year have all been honored by their
survivors

the music that sounded through it has gone through the
air around the earth many times

the shame and violence and fine meals and embraces are
only stories retold retold

not one day of it can be recalled in full

only some mornings and some evenings unrelated to each
other come to mind

was I at my height? fallen to my depth?

it is better not to pretend I said to myself

now is not 35 years ago but only now does it seem terrible
and wonderful

the depth of it below me holds me up

from this height I hover over it seeing the beauty of its
    shape

I am there or a younger I is there amongst the blurred
    details

though I can't land I can at least keep flying

or rather because I can't land I must keep flying

LOCAL HISTORY

walking to the monroe county public library
the sidewalk under crabtrees
still spotted with stains from last autumn's fruit
one empty store three still occupied
all the windows receive and then lose images
of those passing by

next block:
1874 — colored school
1915 — carnegie library (colored school gone)
1970 — library moves
1980 — monroe county history center and museum
    (swallows carnegie library)
all this is documented on signs on metal poles

then the plain geometry of the parking lot
and at the corner overhung by kind trees
the benches where the homeless guys spend part of
    their day
not too often letting out some wounded sarcasm
at one of those passing by on his way
to the monroe county public library

A FIELD OF BOXES

its owner the one who lives far away
the one with an appetite
who made so many of us
he couldn't eat them all

TENDER

when the fire sinks low a little stirring helps
or blowing bent over at its root of coals

the fire rises over itself again
the fire is made of its fuel and my knowledge of fire

half moon first star I wish for those I love
the best of fates or failing that for courage

the cooling after-sunset air slides from
the grassy ridge downhill through the trees

I sit with my back to it and listen to
the early spring carousal of peepers

the night begins to flourish with stars and I think
how bloodroot goldenseal and maidenhair

have all come up today and wonder when
it was that someone of my kind began

to learn to tend a fire how many thousands
of years ago and how it was most likely

the fire itself that taught him so if only
he held attention close on it all night

THIS SHINING

this life so rich with coincidence
anticipation falls apart into shards of urges
the heart's long trial of saying do! and don't!
its bidding and forbidding
ends in a scatter of experience
unrepeatable
accidental

this place the hovering clouds sigh over
as their shadows plot on the meadows
the upper winds' motions
this earth to lie on weighted
by our experience as by a dew
to rise from weightless evaporates

this sky heaving with storms or empty and glaring
these stars piercing distances amazing in their extremity
the prophecies we pattern on their conjunctions
if they seem true our desires seem true
if they lie our hearts lie
if fate had a face it would be modest and regular
it would sympathize itself with our world
anything could happen next or after next

I am as close as your hand when you read this
if everything I've told you were piled together
it would fit in a hole the size a dog could go in
if you look up you see the wind shuffling
thunderheads and a body of birds
your way over the horizon and at night you can plot
a clutch of stars shifting very ancient but still shining

POEM ENDING WITH WHAT I JUST ATE

record the seasons
record the trace of light across your thoughts
record the way a face becomes a fact
record breakfast the ditches a doorway
record what you have time for

don't worry about the excluded mass
of sensations objects memories feelings
flying digging swimming creatures
some unmentioned star some forgotten act
this mass is in its own unsaid poem
so abstract that it only touches
the edge of your thoughts
as you pick up your bowl of oatmeal

ALMOST A YEAR SINCE MY MOTHER DIED

some restless leaves fill the air
with their shifting traffic

I look for a sorrow I think I must have
misplaced so necessary does it seem
to follow on certain losses

someone somewhere is having a hurricane
here the leaves let loose of their twigs
and stirred by the wind come to earth
gently like birds landing

offshore the hurricane stirs the deep for monsters
but we have only this next layer of leaves
washing down to feed the soil
a natural thing like the progression:
"I have parents" "I have a mother" "I . . ."

from AMD #20

THE GREAT WORKS

Reading one of the Great Works that you find annoying, you realize that the works you like would annoy someone else. His likes and yours cancel each other, and all that remains is the shouting to be heard. So much arguing between friends may be what we mean by "Great," as sure a sign as the raised hairs. What we mean by "Works" is that it fails its promise every time and must be re-done, with help from everybody.

12/13/12

the squirrels' efforts
look like toys
their search
into the leafmold
an ancient play

first to see
the possibilities
they picked out
one thing
hidden in the others

to make much of
the way anyone
filling his mouth could pretend
it is an art of comedy
to eat

ABOUT THE FAMOUS COUNTRY

the leaves cover it
the respiration of anthills warms it
a house built there
has no front door
all its doors are back doors

there are roads no one uses
there are rocks placed to show
where its famous men paused
before their greatest effort

a spider walking along
one of the twigs there
has no thought in it has only
a pattern to make visible that
its brain a couple of fibers hides

REPETITION

those who in their agony of loss
die of grief make another grief

WONDERFUL

at the doctor's office
the sick are lining up by the fish tank
they finger the insurance cards in their pockets
and watch fins flicking at water
to maintain a stable posture

one very large very dark fish
with irregular blotches on its sides
lies so still on a fake rock
it looks like a fake rock too

its absence of movement does not betray
the fact that it is looking out at the patients
why do some of them lean on
those contraptions made of sticks?
what makes some of them cough?

it must be a signal they give to the others
to move for they do
move gently away from the ones with sticks
nature is wonderful thinks the fish

SAYING MORE

cold air on my skin as it leaves me alert pleases
dirt is innocent of all the crimes thrust into it
deep inside the stone is a trace of the water that made it
a saying repeated may become useful because of repeated
    saying

water repeats itself over the stones
skin: crimes and pleasures
what is useful to us thrusts through dirt
a cold saying airs itself to the alert

become innocent repeating pleasures
deep water is cold water
crimes themselves trace their making
sayings as repeated as stones in dirt

THE TOWN

the town with its mildly hilly north side
its flat and flood prone south and all its
tired crossroads which
the sun passes through every day
tidy angles of light changing calmly minute to minute
everything is a system the mayor proclaims
even what I am not telling you
by telling you that

a cat gray broad headed scarred from fights
has wandered behind the license branch
on his way to his favorite trash can favorite
not so much for the trash as for the rats
he sees the sun and thinks
ha! you have one but I
have two
yellow eyes

the grocer in his long white apron
is the only one listening to the mayor
but really he is waiting for him to move
so he can sweep there too
farmers and their wives are coming in
from all directions bearing broken machinery
and shopping lists
everyone must get busy

an old lady across the alley
from the cat's favorite trash
looks at him over her back yard
from her seat on her back porch
things have changed the songs she knows best
no one sings out loud anymore
they hum them now as if ashamed to be heard
a little whisper of song works to speed memory
which is slow and stiff and gets stuck in one place
that cat thinks he's so quick and always will be
she says to herself but I have far more years than him
and I know what he doesn't

1937

the Ohio in flood
my parents have not yet met

my father is a young man
trying to work out a way
to avoid being a farmer
and just beginning to
fail at one alternative after another
he has not yet reached the last one
and failed at it too
which will force him to show
his true excellence

my mother is still in school
and probably already as angrily unsatisfied
as she will be later
probably as funny and beguiling
as greedy of attention
as sharp-tongued and sad
as eager to tell a story
probably already dreaming of mountains and cities

far to the south of them
another Ohio lays on top of the first
together they escape the banks
that have always defined "Ohio River"
and run over the surrounding lands
ruining homes and scraping away crops
killing and exiling many

for ages people have preferred to live by rivers
it offers many advantages
especially as settlements grow larger
they crowd their houses near the water
they send and receive by it
they get their news off it
and from time to time this happens
and they get their sorrow too

what did my mother and father hear about it?
a disaster so far away it couldn't touch them
but close enough there must have been much talk
probably their knowledge of it was slight
and quickly drifted to the back of the mind
life can be hard enough to account for
without worrying about others' heartaches

STONE SYMPATHY

this large rock in the abandoned field
its back arching up like one stooped
to pick there and a crack showing
made by time and sun and sun and sun
looks like it's waiting to pull
its hands and feet from the dirt
and trudge off to find its mountain again
or its seabed or wherever it came from
but its weight holds it fast in the field
to take on its back the full blast of weather
and sun and time and time and time

ANOTHER KIND OF WIND I REMEMBER

the whirlwinds that used to come
while the hay was being raked
and grab a piece of windrow
and pull it up like a thread
of spiderweb being torn from its base
by some hasty animal running in fear
from a movement in the brush that was
only the wind stirring the branches
only the wind

IRONY WATER

the irony water I drank in youth
made a red stain wherever a pipe dripped
as though our wells had tapped
earth's own blood

odorless tasteless water
made me feel pale
our water gave me
an iron constitution

that's what I thought
on those hot days I went
straight to the wellhouse
sweating from the fields

from AMD #21

HE ADDRESSES HIS SOUL

if what hurt my flesh
or made my heart drop
a beat or brought my rage
to my mouth never
touched you

you must be
still as good as the day I got you
as round as polished
still humming the same note
and neither stronger nor weaker
for all the years

my sins don't stain you
my scars don't mark you
my despair weighs nothing
when you lift it to test it

but still my heartless companion
when I look in the mirror
of the years I see
more and more
we look alike

VOYAGER

wander on between the stars
the wind of solar flares at your back
nothing stops you nothing slows you down
you speed through interstellar black
where nothing can come back

the sea where you now swim has taken in
the discharged hopes and loves from lives
long broken up and has received
a crowd of solitudes from all earth's time
pains that have forgot the bodies
that made them float out there with you
on all the exhaled sighs
of our little system of rocks and fire

no orbit can snare you again
you cruise past heavens that lost their last believers
back when some empire fell just short of utopia
you speed where fainting funeral organ tones
fuel prayers stretched out to transparency
still seeking their target and
still followed by their second thoughts

failed harvest predictions keep trying
to find a place of abundance to land
ownership plus and slavery minus
have finally come to zero
where you are — oh voyager
wander still and hear our plea:

go on between the stars
go on in interstellar black
where nothing slows you down
where nothing can come back

OUR HISTORY

history wouldn't miss us
if we got separated from it
it's rolled past us all our lives
not looking our way

not that we haven't noticed it:
far from its core we felt
all its peripheral effects
its effluents determined
where we lived and how

we got drunk we loved
we tried a move
argued failed resumed
sat one evening in the yard
thinking how the day had passed
insignificantly
even the sweat squeezed
from us by our actions
hardly stank

no books about us —
others endured or triumphed
made fortunes or invented
while we have made
no discoveries greater than
how the day's passing
can be delayed
just by noticing it

FALL RAIN EARLY MORNING

like fingertips ticking on the strings
each drop can be heard for itself
and together they are a kind of music
fostered by a shared rhythm

the dark is when we listen best
if all the lights are put out and I stand
at the kitchen window looking east
straight into the trees gathered there

I know I will see nothing at all
but my ears will sharpen sliding
across one drop after another as if
ordinary rain were the first or only rain

THE FOUR DIRECTIONS

toward the cold
toward the heat
toward daybreak
toward night

is
was
will be
might

to me
to you
to them
to no one

I dream
I remember
I wish for
I wish away

WHERE YOU ARE

the wilderness
under your feet always
even if it seems sealed away
by the street

a wilderness of bedrock
under the streets and
the striving of buildings
rock born of the wilderness of time

and the air
touching your face is
forever the wild air that runs
its own will over the city

YEARS LATER

close to the house
the trees hold out
their cold fingers
to its warmth

the wind makes
a hollow sound and
presses your eyes
unwilling closed

in twenty years
it has not been
this cold
they say

twenty years of
lonely wandering
for the cold to
find his way back

he tracks in behind him
an empty clarity and
you can't help noticing
or is it remembering

how deep the zero sinks
how close the dry sky
with its piece of moon
and white stars

THEORY

everything opened up in fire
that rush rush
as of wings beating

the great world's dark breast
was newly speckled with stars
that twitched over a heart

driving all onward and the wings
opening and closing like flames
made their own space to fly in

A LIFE IN MUSIC

busy to make music
how he got swept along in it
the only organized thing
his life ever held

when not thrown over
or run out when at home
for a bit between disasters
his fingers worked fast

to his instrument
and a few friends at times
or strangers also got busy
at it with him

hewed close to the line
the sounds were laid along
with him and till quite late
enclosed in music all was joy

STORIES

There was once a man who had been told no stories.
He was first and had not been told of anywhere remote
and strange, nor of lives familiar and real and common.
He had not even, due to his position at the start of telling
things, been told raw lies, poor devil. He was first, and so
tried to tell when it came to him to do it a story like
the world and found that lies, above all obvious ones told
with real heart and an appeal for belief, his children —
wide-eyed and so trusting — were most fond of.

WHITMAN AMONGST THE WILLOWS

old and wrestling
them because bending their limbs
with his strengthens him

and his desire
to live
is given a spur
by the way the sappy boughs
flex like muscled arms

the water nearby
purrs along its channel
drops of sweat
moisten his white beard
when the young trunk is pressed
to the ground it springs back
from his hands

and the light filtered
through the narrow leaves
speckles his brow
creased by the work

WHILE WE SLEPT

the storms while we slept with their racket
and plunging creeks dangers of lightning
trees shaken nests overturned and drenching
that washed away yesterday and with it
yesterday's frailest blossoms
have run their course and rest now
against some far off mountain slope that receives them
as it received their grandparents' grandparents
the place where storms no longer have to try
but can set themselves down in a gentle rain

the storms while we slept were like a dream
of a dream so far back in the mind
they were not even an alarm or minor trouble
but only the sound of sleep itself yes they were
like a hand that no matter how hard its work has made it
is still softer than the earth tough enough to bear all
and its strokes do not rouse us from but only deepen
    our sleep

from AMD #22

NIGHT QUIET SHELTER

checking the progress of the night
by measuring it against my breath

the moon past full
begins to hide her face again

the shy gesture hushes us all
those who can shelter themselves

where the wind can't reach
dark homes where heartbeats

fall together like shavings
gathered for a nest

11/14/14

A dusting, or as my grandmother used to say, "a skift" of snow fell last night. It is cold this morning, but the sun is bright enough to erase the snow wherever it can reach. The shadows of the larger tree trunks save the snow from the sun. Bright bands of white on the ground. The shadows have cast their own shadows. In white.

I JUST WANT TO SAY

I am reputed to _____
I am refuted, too
I had a good reputation
_____ destroyed my refutation

during the Counter-Refutation
many enduring works of art
were placed in rooms
resigned for that purpose

PROFESSIONS

the care of the farmer
for the animals he will empty

the scholar's eyes which read
where nothing seemed written

FOUR SIMPLE OBSERVATIONS

1.
you need your fields
they were not there from the first
but you will need them till the last

2.
the mistakes in music
are not shameful
they are another music coming in

3.
the tool in your hand now
made by other tools other hands
descends from the first stone lifted
to strike another stone

4.
there is flame
that shapely
that bright
motion

THE FIRST APPEARANCE OF LIFE

obviously the first trick
is to learn how to die

a clump of molecules
slightly slimy
falling to pieces

then reattaching each piece
to its neighbor
only to disassemble again
over and over it does this

and teaches the elegant move
to those nearby and similar
the second is to forget perfect order
when reconnecting — thus evolution —
the third is to eat your neighbor

THE SUMMER WE HAD ALL THE RAIN

it was May-cool deep into July
our ankles were never dry
puddles were never empty
it seemed ungrateful to be thirsty
but nonetheless we kept drinking

a leaf battered off its tree
floated down the creek down the river
it was enjoying the travels it had thought
it would never be able to manage
it noticed snakes on the banks
long branches caught against the bridges' legs
nights thickened by clouds

this time tomorrow I'll be
swept up in the barge traffic on the great river
I don't care that I'm waterlogged
and never going home
I'll lie on my back and drift
the current is as good as a breeze to move me
and the river holds me up
as well as a branch would

AUTOBIOGRAPHY VOL. VI

night stops breathing
then she starts up again

she is bothered by me
by having to look after
what I have given up to her

P for instance
his last moment spent
fighting a cold hard rain
for control of his motorcycle
and losing
laying it down in front of a semi
unable to swerve
(poor driver)

or D who finally realized
what all his friends and family knew
his cult leader was a liar
he'd wasted his gift for belief
humiliating
hung himself in his father's garage

night looks after them
and I look up at the night
have I participated in lies?
have I pushed my luck?
obviously so but

without serious consequence up to now
which leaves me as one of the lucky bereft
here to bother the night
who should be used to it by now

SEPTEMBER

has saved scraps of paper
with notes written on them
to be organized later

it lives in a tent made of photographs
recent travels school days long gone
a group of friends smiling around a table
loaded with plates dirtied
with shards of a meal
glasses with dripping sides
the smiles for the moment only
but all of it only a picture
of a table of friends of shards
of smiles

it is a month that can't recall but tries
rises with the sun has nothing to do
bothers its friends plays an old tune
but breaks off halfway

it is getting along just fine
never complains oh maybe
just a little about the dry mouth
and why the afternoons have to be
so hot when the nights are perfectly cool

WORDS ON THE RIVER

on the river the crafts
floating have been given names
and the people guiding them have names too
and there are words for direction
time of day weather state of being
of the river

all this language floating on the river
and the river has nothing to do with it
it cares nothing for words won't speak
continuously carves lower and wider
swells shrinks turns slows speeds
and says nothing is not a language
anyone has ever learned

oh of course we say it is murmuring or
exclaim that it rages but we know nothing
but our metaphors for it not its deep intentions
or unconscious drift downward
we can't get in it even once without talking about it

from AMD #23

untitled

my broken backed books
so many years
only my fingers swept
the dust of them

so much time
like a field of wheat
stretching backwards
to another field

I remember that old sickle
in the broken down barn
it outlasted
the last arm that swung it

lay there in the loose straw
for boys to play with
long past its sharpness
exact curve rough handle

JULY AGAIN

the nights as they are
plain thoughts
open with movements so pure
they seem static
the days messy with light

show every action
in stubborn witness
the dusk held between them
is both stillness and motion
as seeming to be lifted
just by holding its wings open

the heron out of shadows
makes its flight home
over waters roughened
by fish striking
at flies and striders
one last run and then night

THE TREES ARE STILL FULLY CLOTHED
IN LEAVES

but soon they will drop them to the ground
the tallest the ones near a century old
will stand there naked and boney

like skinny old men in a doctor's office
waiting patiently as long as need be
for someone to come along with a gown

like skinny old men who are closer
to falling down than rising up
speechless lost inside themselves

but seeming to tower over the rest of us
because all the years they've lived through
are there in the shape of them

RURAL

the red barns and the white ones
pigeons' cool voices from the rafters

weeds and grasses in the ditches
ordered rows of crops in the fields

during the long dry spell
every little use of the roads

sifts the dust of them airborne
to powder the growth of the ditches

dust on the wild grasses' bent blades
grain on the beds of wagons rolling

along the roads from fields to barn
everything rides on the back of something else

the farmer's sons ride on the tractors
he shouts to them over the engine noise

inside a day the necessary work is done
everything is inside something else

stubble in the stripped fields
grain in the barn with the pigeons

the whole load of summer rains
inside a seed gathered up and piled with others

all of it inside time and
time itself inside the creatures it made

NOTE TO SELF

Last day of the year, last light of day, a walk in the woods. Like any other day, any other walk. The strong wind earlier today pushed down an old dead sumac and helped the tall tulip trees shed some old branches. The newly-fallen lying next to the long-fallen in the leaf litter. Sedge grasses here and there in a spray of green ribbons tight to the ground. Traffic noise in the distance, people hurrying to some party or to get safely home before the partying begins. The year about to start contains the centenary of my father's birth. His birth set mine in motion, as a distant consequence. Mine led to the writing of this note to myself, just as it will lead to every bland or extraordinary moment or event to come. Until it all falls out of existence in the space of a breath. All that line of days of two lifetimes ending in a nothing, some of them having been passed in devoted attention.

ON THE WEST SIDE OF TOWN

those many crows gathered in the trees
surrounding the extensive parking lot
that serves the strip mall on the west side of town
caw from all sides from the trees from the air
some swing into action and overfly the lot
most maintain their perches firmly set
backs straight and shoulders squared
it is early sunday morning only a few cars
the 24 hour grocery store consumes one
individual shopper at a time and emits
each later they mostly carry just one
plastic bag each some necessity or
imagined necessity drove them here in this hour of
only a glimmer signaling that the sun is about to rise
from behind the dense cloud cover that buries it
the lights set high over the parking lot
are still on one crow flies in and out
through them notched wingtips silhouetted
against the light gray sky speaking to
his brethren solemn in the nearby trees
who answer by some order the crows know
to follow but the people below them walking
from or to their cars can't interpret or is it
better to say they ignore the crows having
no interest in them or their caws or other doings

ECONOMY

spend a thousand
owe a thousand
earn a thousand
want a thousand

a thousand listen
each word
each sound
set on the two ears
of each listener

so now its
two thousand!
just like that!

and there
on the bench
at a slight distance
from the thousand

sits
eating something
wrapped in paper

one
only one

from AMD #24

5/5/17

dreamed all night
under continuous rain

in one of them I said
flooding is certain tomorrow
though I don't know to whom or why

rain had come even to my dreams
the faces were cloudy but the rain was clear
dream after dream and towards the end of one
I dreamed that I wondered how it is that I am surprised

at what people in my dreams say to me
after all who but me tells them what to say?
it was raining when I fell asleep raining when I woke
rattle of rain all night on the roof and my first words
    on waking
were spoken to myself: it will flood today and
    tomorrow downstream

LAZARUS LAUGHS

a fly has landed
on the back of his hand

it turns around and around
pulls back its head for a wider look

and stamps its feet
to test the flesh

is it death or life?
the fly is discomposed

and Lazarus laughs
he can't help himself

he is in spasms
the joke is on the fly

FLOWERS ON THE GRAVES OF THE OVERDOSED

the wind shifts through them
and they move shaking
their generosity of color
against the gray stone
where the name is fixed
like sorrow dancing before memory

the frail bones are packed in dirt
we visit them as though we could
still visit the person
but the bones are not the person
who was taken from us violently
I meant to say softly
by deception

the person is now in our minds only
invulnerable there...

the red flower of a living mouth
memory makes it bloom again
memory is like the clouds
hovering on the scene
continually recreated
seeming close but actually at a distance
not subject to harm
as is the easily torn
and prone to withering flesh
that makes up the form of flowers

untitled

sleeping
then waking

working
then resting

drinking
then pissing

loving
then hating

listening
then talking

walking
then standing

wondering
then knowing

leaving
then returning

breathing
then

LATE JANUARY

cold rain all day

we have one kind of winter and then another

the fog many mornings obscures the way

I am in my tenth day of mourning
for someone who died four years ago

found out ten days ago so is his death
new or something in the past

perfect for this is such a day:

rain that never stops drumming
and an impenetrable sky

I can look at old sheets of paper
look up old messages

I can hear certain music again
search out photographs

I can get on with my day

I can hope that this winter the miserable cold
never returns the roads remain unblocked

I can use the unblocked roads anytime I wish
to go anywhere I want

I will not think that there is in my town right now
some poor fucker who never quite trusts himself

who looks ahead and thinks how long

who looks at the rain and thinks how much more

whose thoughts are bent toward the impenetrable

and are sweet and angry and like no other

WRITING FOR NO ONE

is in a language so lost
no chisel has ever touched it

writing for no one is done in the dark
and will be read ditto

the peeps chirrs and scratching
heard in the background

are themselves an opaque literature
inspired by forgetfulness

at midnight the world closes
around itself

circle inside circle
writer disappears reader disappears

the zodiac is torn from its stories
and becomes geometrical proof

everything is gone but the purity
of the speechless world

IN THE MIDDLE

The Check 'N Go, the martial arts academy, Low Bob's
Tobacco Outlet and Vape Store, and Carson's Bar-B-Q,
which promises dine-in and carryout, but just now is
closed because they're at the Owen County Fair. Hope
their business is good there, but no Bar-B-Q for me today.
The place I'm in is mainly parking lot, with a Big Lots off
to the side. Big Lots is always open when you expect it
to be, and they sell Cafe Bustelo for three-eighty-five per
ten ounce vacuum sealed pack. What this life is, is
satisfaction mixed with disappointment. The nation is on
edge. Are we lost, or is this simply what we're really like?
I am an American poet, heir to pride and silliness, here
in the middle of the nation trying to figure it all out.
You can never figure it all out, but you can meet all kinds
of people whose situations you recognize even if the face
is unfamiliar, in the checkout line at Big Lots.

LEFT BEHIND

One of the gods was left behind when the others went.
Unemployed, permanently. Found a cheap place to rent,
bought discount clothes, got a beer belly and let his face go
shaggy. Took up smoking. He thinks he is unknown, but we
only pretend not to recognize him. To make him
comfortable, so he stays amongst us.

POEM COMPLETED ON MY 68TH BIRTHDAY

1.
it was strange but
I was stranger

I meant to say strong but strange will do

2.
the sun leaps out of the east every morning
but never surprises us
it's always pursuing its own track of the day before

the sun is in one spot at a time
but night is all over the place
its little noises make us jump

I have we have our own everleaping sun inside
our own jumpy dark

never mind what the world shakes at us to threaten
look inside
if you want to know what's making you move

3.
like a dog leashed to an erratic master
I must pull us back on track

I am hiding here as eric rensberger
who is stranger now for having survived his troubles

how will he know when he's written enough?
by his palms cramping
by his tongue limping

he knows what a dog knows
about tugging

he knows what the sun knows
about falling

and he holds up writing as that example
to show the world a puppet a human made
and all that jerks when you pull its strings

WET DAY

what if
in this heavy rain
there is between the drops packed together
a hollow drop
an empty drop
a drop made of air or nothing

and it all falls at the same time
rain and hollow rain
and it all runs off of us

trickle and hollow trickle
seep and hollow seep
stream and hollow stream
river and hollow river
tides and hollow tides
world and hollow world

WATCHING FOR THE STORM

as if it were any use
as if we were still in a world
the gods imagined for us
and peopled with signs
I eye the sky while I
check the wind with my body

so much to see
before it lands
so many kinds of dark
where what comes next is

the strong rule the weak
with no relief
power cannot sustain itself
on truth

the wind is steadily rising
clouds crowd each other aside

as if it were any use
I try to tell one cloud from another
and look for which comes forward fastest

10/17/18

all travelers tonight
whether the wind slows or speeds you
whether you are returning to or going farther from home
whether you watch or turn away

that house you are passing is mine
and inside it I patiently name
all the gods I can remember
and wait to see if any still speaks

there is an act of looking I can only do from a distance
and I want someone to look that way at me
from a distance each of us is fit
to a moment and a place worth knowing

and from that place believing in fate
and believing that fate can change
are the same belief the one that launches prayers
with a speed like light glancing off water

from AMD #25

DEMOCRACY:

death
and infidelity
at every step

he worried furious
that what was so loved
was so under threat

with age
came not wisdom
as he pretended

but weariness
that took away fury
but couldn't touch

the memory of love
who he had loved
and what

that is the curious thing
how fury to affirm
to protect

left him
though what he loved
remained under threat

READING

The article said the public figure said his intentions had been misrepresented by those saying negative things about him. I was reading in a hurry, because I was fundamentally uninterested in the story but thought it was something I should want to know more about. Because I was speed reading, I read "intentions" as "intestines": "they misrepresented my intestines." This was so close to making sense that I paused and re-read the complaint about what was being said that was quoted in the article I was not really interested in. And I thought about what misrepresented intestines might look like. I took a sip of coffee, realizing that my reading was no longer speedy, and that it had been slowed down in order to contemplate not something hard to understand or beautiful to read, but an absurdity that both confused and stimulated the imagination. Why do I push myself to read so fast so early in the morning. I thought about my intentions

POEM ENDING WITH AN APOLOGY
FOR GLOBAL WARMING

I've held up well so far
all the noise I let myself hear
and the truth I won't listen to

taken together could be
the reason why I keep claiming
to know everything worth knowing

and at the same time manage
to plead ignorance
whenever I need to

my full attention to one instant
chosen for its emptiness
makes the others go by fast

I thus participate in my own
distraction so that when I see more than
one room of the house falling apart

it seems easy to say oh hell
why not burn the whole thing down
as so many have done before me

autumn has fallen on us
exhaustedly
wanting it all to be done with

August was dry
September went a pinch beyond that
now things turn brown and drop

if I spit on the ground
it's not disrespect
I'm trying to make amends

PRESS RELEASE

I did not mean
and I did not imply that
I did not say that
I had held my tongue

there were no assertions and no denials

not even a twitch or a shrug
escaped me
to make it seem I had anything
to reveal or to hold back

it is not even clear
that there was a person there
similar to me or me exactly
who meant and said nothing

ON READING IN THE MIDDLE
OF THE NIGHT

time stops at 3 a.m.
nothing moves but everything is quietly alive

a sleepless wind runs over silent roads
those alert enough to evade their dreams

read the night as a history
written in fantastic letters moving like slow beasts

each line leads to all the others and
any meaning is huddled deep inside the herd

hidden there with the proof that if
everyone is alone now 3 a.m. never ends

WHAT WE KNOW NOW

we know how dangerous we are to each other
how we need each other
we know as we didn't know before how much we live
    in our hands
how we make our place in the world with them
how we need and touch and need and touch
now we can't stop thinking about our hands
now the things we've said with them are new again
for instance give me a hand
or living hand to mouth

we now know that when we are forbidden to touch our faces
our faces come alive with a longing for our hands
an unbearable itch only fingers can ease

and we know now as we know our own hands who it is
    that is most necessary to us
and we know a new meaning of far away
that is only a different way of saying apart
and in that longing for the necessary one we know each
    other
we know the distraught distance each feels
we know how we need each other

WASHING MY HANDS

sliding into each other's pockets
the deep gap between fingers
the shallow cups of the palms
they seem to know each other so well
these servants of my intentions

when I used them to get knowledge of the world
to find things in the dark for instance
or to measure warmth or smoothness
I thought no more of them than of a tool
and I have I confess shouted at them

for their clumsiness
when I wanted to put my own failure
at a distance from me
as though we were no part of each other
and they could carry the blame

but now I feel through them how warm warm
water is and how it pleases to slide
them over and over each other
I wash them as a way to care for myself
and to feel a kind of prayerful blessing

I recite in only twenty seconds
the names of those I have loved most
and try to believe in my hands
in what they still have left to do
in the world cleanly and with great skill

INCOMPLETE NARRATIVE

1.
fell to the floor
and couldn't lever up
but there was a chair nearby
so got up that way

2.
no chair nearby
neighbor brought one
all OK

3.
no chair no neighbor bare room
put his ear to the floor to listen
he could hear a chair below
scraping the floor when it moved

4.
sat in the chair
and the chair fell over

on the floor
still in the chair
I wish I could fly he said

THE CENTER OF MY LIFE

The center of my life is not here. It is away. It has been
ever and always away. I'm not complaining. It's the same
for everyone. The center of my life is distant but
imaginable, so you can never forget that you are away
from it. We try to replace the center with religion, politics,
drinking, obsessive learning, love of family. This last one
is especially effective, until you reflect that there is another
family out there, also yours but you don't know each other.
The center of your family could be anyone you pass, or it
could be one amongst the crowds of people centuries past.
Or perhaps you are a genetic sport, and you will have no
true relatives till the same mutation appears randomly at
some point in the unfathomable depths of the future,
that one difference from others that makes you the same
as one or several who will live henceafterwards, for whom
you will be only a trace of bone chips and dust under a rock.

WHY OUR DISASTERS MEAN SO MUCH TO US

it's our chance to learn what can't be saved for later
our way of sowing heroes into the earth
our compass points through the landscape of history
our chance to recover from the weakness our
    certainties have smothered us with

our disasters are like a sudden spray of light
making the night sky live like us
startling and gone in a breath

when they are so remote as to be someone else's disasters
all we can do is sympathize with strangers
but in the light of our own disasters
we see ourselves and each other
and what it is we stand to lose

AT MORNING

the world eats words
some mine
to make itself
into the fattest prayer

the light stretches
toward me as if
listening
stretches so close
that what it hears
must matter

8/25/20

up by the house
it's hot and steamy
even my fingernails sweat

but in the woods
and all the way downhill
cooler and cooler

till at the bottom
standing in the wash there
on the cool dry stones

it's like I'm in the basement
of the woods
maybe there's a basement to everything

something below us
where everything is tolerable
where we can go if we need to

from AMD #26

9/24/20

days of contempt
dry
black dirt gone ash colored
you can imagine smoke anywhere

are we falling
or is something falling on us
what held the whole thing up
has failed

the heart tires
straining amidst trials that test it
to the breaking point

we feel it all day long
and as possible as it is to go on
we hope it is as possible to stop

TWO THOUGHTS

1.
what it says
about us
that we sing
when sorrowful
make music
for funerals
lay a line
of melody
over the grave

2.
the bands of rock
color by color
one era atop
another
our most
ancient ancestors
turned to stone
and the swamp
they passed time in
now hardened too

and over all
layer by layer
remains of
the hardships
of each generation
succeeding
the prior one

what pressure
they must feel
those who came first
under the weight
of all those
troubled times
that followed them

10/26/20

after the rainy days finally come
the ground fills

it gets heavier
and stops looking like dust

the news is bad and relentless as rain
I fill with anxiety

my mind feels heavier
my body is clumsy

when I talk to myself
to explain away the fear

or plan how to live with it
my speech is slow and hesitating

it keeps on raining
I fear the future

there must be a way to understand things
that would soothe me

but if words were all it took to understand
I would have stopped trying by now

LIFE WELL LIVED

make a world
lose a world

and again:

make a world
lose a world

that's your life

child's world
made and lost

youth's world
made and lost

old one to whom
loss is familiar

they say you
only live once

but:

you lose
many times

ONE WHO DIDN'T KNOW

sometimes the malice of the world
sings to itself:

the wheels shriek
wind picks up
one must pay
close attention to know
is it distant thunder
or explosives?

sometimes it buries itself
so deep in the hearts of the people
that there's nothing to hear
it can't be noticed at all
until the moment it has chosen

sometimes it flits
from thing to thing so much
you don't know where it is
from moment to moment

the last time the ground shook
there was one who didn't know

he lay on the rug saying
I'm shaking
I'm shaking
I'm shaking

to him
the world was fine
it was poor he
who was in tremors

SKILL

after many revisions
this is what I have to say

silence weighs more than speech

the stories we tell
are told from one loneliness to another

metaphor: one thing is
now another
so neither is
anymore itself

my pen touching paper
seeks a balance point

there is a skill to keeping it there
and another to striking a line
through everything

ELEGY NUMBER ___

after a life is gone has been done
inside each second
is something of him waiting for us

like a face you almost see
in a drop of water

so tiny a thing to leave behind
he won't even miss it

A DEITY

The god of disappearances, worshipped in an enormous
room stacked with stuff, where people filing through the
mounds find poets living on grants given to enumerate all
the things deposited there. There is so much of it that no
one thing can be proved to be gone. It could always be at
the bottom of the next pile or on top of that heap. It's as
though everything that comes here has disappeared because
it can't be found in all the clutter, but also exists forever
for it cannot be shown to be lost. And in the murmur of
poets' prayers all the enumerations sound like elegies.

GOODBYE

I go outside
build a small fire
sit close enough to it
the sweat runs down
off my face

I don't cry
not once
I think about you
but I don't cry
not once

the fire
falls apart
the embers crumble
the smoke
goes up to heaven

the world is so old
sometimes
and we just
stay so young
it hurts

ADAGE

if poetry makes anything clear
it's how hard it is
to say what we've lost

Eric Rensberger grew up in Elkhart County, Indiana, and has lived for most of his life in Monroe County. He has been involved in Bloomington's local poetry community since arriving there in 1979. He is the author of several chapbooks and has been published in anthologies of Bloomington area poets, as well as appearing in local or regional magazines. He has self-published through his website, which can be found at www.ericrensbergerpoetry.net. That site is the primary home for his ongoing chronological series Account of My Days.

This project was made possible, in part, by generous support from the Osage Arts Community.

Osage Arts Community provides temporary time, space and support for the creation of new artistic works in a retreat format, serving creative people of all kinds — visual artists, composers, poets, fiction and nonfiction writers. Located on a 152-acre farm in an isolated rural mountainside setting in Central Missouri and bordered by ¾ of a mile of the Gasconade River, OAC provides residencies to those working alone, as well as welcoming collaborative teams, offering living space and workspace in a country environment to emerging and mid-career artists. For more information, visit us at www.osageac.org

Osage Arts Community